What Your Colleagues

"Readers will have 7 BILLION reasons to be HOF___ to influence their students' behavior as well as their future. Cathleen's personal journey toward understanding the power of hope comes alive through her heartfelt storytelling. Her unique perspective as a mom, foster parent, teacher, colleague, and researcher will draw you in as she shares the science of hope and offers valuable tools for the classroom. This book couldn't come at a better time for teachers yearning to help their students develop the mindset and perseverance needed to overcome trauma."

—Helen Barrier
High incidence disabilities coordinator
Virginia Tech Training and Technical Assistance Center
Blacksburg, VA

"In The School of Hope, *author Cathleen Beachboard provides the blueprint for educators to create environments founded on healing by shaping a space that fosters a sense of safety. Teachers can spark hope for students and colleagues despite the challenges and trauma experienced during the pandemic. This book is a must-read for all educators who want to foster school cultures of hope."*

—Barbara Bray
Creative learning strategist, podcast host, speaker, coach, co-author of
Make Learning Personal and *How to Personalize Learning,*
and author of *Define Your Why*

"This book provides research, anecdotal information, and practical activities and forms to help school staff build HOPE for students and staff who suffer from past or continuing trauma. This book and the movement that it recommends is useful for all levels of educators and greater community members from PreK to collegiate programs. Preservice teachers should have this information in order to prepare for today's students who may have been out of the traditional classroom for months. As a nation, we could be facing the fact that almost every student has encountered some form of trauma due to the COVID pandemic. Many have lost family members, such as grandparents, and will be dealing with fear and grief for some time to come. We know that creating safe and caring classrooms and school communities are the foundations for academic achievement."

—Carrie Jane Carpenter
ELA, SS, and reading educator, Oregon Teacher of the Year 2003

"This book is both inspiring and practical! So many students have faced adversity and this book equips educators to come alongside them, encourage them, increase their resilience, and give them the tools to thrive. However, the incredible impact will not be limited to students. Educators, administrators, and clinicians can all benefit from the wisdom and guidance found here. What a much-needed, timely resource for us all!"

—Holly N. Deemer
Clinical psychologist and psychology instructor
Liberty University
Lynchburg, VA

"This book is absolutely needed, even more so with the increase in mental health issues as a result of the COVID-19 pandemic. Even pre-pandemic, mental health needs and trauma were raising concerns of educators about how to best meet the increasing needs of our students. This will be a valuable resource for educators. As a principal, I could see it as an ideal faculty book study."

—Jessica Johnson
Principal
Dodgeland School District, WI

"This text marries the important roles of parent and teacher as it describes the strategies and resources we need to help children overcome trauma and navigate their way through difficult situations at home and at school."

—Susan Stone Kessler
Executive principal
Hunters Lane High School
Nashville, TN

"Hope is the intangible yet indispensable ingredient students and teachers need to persist and prevail during these challenging times. In this important new book, Cathleen Beachboard explains the psychology of hope and how it can be cultivated in schools. For educators and others seeking to instill optimism despite the challenges we face about the future, this book will be a source of inspiration and a guide for how we can make hope a resource for the students who need it most."

—Pedro A. Noguera
Dean of Rossier School of Education and Distinguished Professor of Education
University of Southern California
Los Angeles, CA

"This book offers a compelling message of H.O.P.E. for educators across all disciplines in moving from an idea to implementation. It's a quick read filled with personal stories and experiences and it is a great time-saving guide for busy educators. Self-care plans and practical strategies for meeting students where they are and assisting them with social and emotional needs create and instill hope within your organization. The School of Hope is one handy tool that will not be stored on a shelf and will enhance the culture and performance of one's organization."

—Debra Paradowski
Associate principal/administrator
Arrowhead Union High School
Hartland, WI

"This book provides educators with strategies that can support students in learning that the negative impact of traumatic experiences doesn't have to control their lives. While teachers may not have backgrounds in developing the social emotional skills of students and colleagues, all teachers are able to ensure a classroom and school environment that nurtures acceptance and hope for all."

—Ernie Rambo
Programs coordinator
Nevada National Board Professional Learning Institute

"The School of Hope *is a timely and important book. Near the end of this book, the author claims that 'changing the world, changing school cultures, and changing classrooms starts with hope.' How true! And this book helps us to understand* why *it is true as well as* how *we can go about creating the hopeful schools and cultures we need in our society today. I highly recommend this book not only for educators but also for anyone interested in living a hope-filled life and instilling hope within others."*

—Jeffrey Zoul
Author, speaker, leadership coach, publisher, and president of ConnectEDD

The School of Hope

I dedicate this book to you who open it. You who seek knowledge. You who constantly search for the best tools and strategies to help yourself and others. The world needs more people like you. Share your voice, expertise, and what you learn with others using the hashtag #HOPEforEdu. We are stronger together.

Romans 5:3-4

−C. B.

The School of Hope

The Journey from Trauma and
Anxiety to Achievement,
Happiness, and Resilience

Cathleen Beachboard

FOR INFORMATION:

Corwin

A SAGE Company

2455 Teller Road

Thousand Oaks, California 91320

(800) 233-9936

www.corwin.com

SAGE Publications Ltd.

1 Oliver's Yard

55 City Road

London EC1Y 1SP

United Kingdom

SAGE Publications India Pvt. Ltd.

B 1/I 1 Mohan Cooperative Industrial Area

Mathura Road, New Delhi 110 044

India

SAGE Publications Asia-Pacific Pte. Ltd.

18 Cross Street #10-10/11/12

China Square Central

Singapore 048423

President: Mike Soules

Vice President and Editorial Director: Monica Eckman

Publisher: Jessica Allan

Content Development Editor: Mia Rodriguez

Editorial Intern: Ricardo Rodriguez

Project Editor: Amy Schroller

Copy Editor: Shannon Kelly

Typesetter: C&M Digitals (P) Ltd.

Cover Designer: Candice Harman

Marketing Manager: Olivia Bartlett

Printed in Canada

Library of Congress Cataloging-in-Publication Data

Names: Beachboard, Cathleen, author.

Title: The school of hope : the journey from trauma and anxiety to achievement, happiness, and resilience / Cathleen Beachboard.

Description: Thousand Oaks, California : Corwin, 2022. | Includes bibliographical references and index.

Identifiers: LCCN 2021063072 | ISBN 9781071853849 (paperback) | ISBN 9781071853887 (epub) | ISBN 9781071853870 (epub) | ISBN 9781071853863 (pdf)

Subjects: LCSH: Affective education—United States. | School children—Mental health. | Teachers—Mental health. | Psychic trauma in children. | Student-teacher relationships. | School environment—Psychological aspects.

Classification: LCC LB1072 .B427 2022 | DDC 370.15/34—dc23/eng/20220124

LC record available at https://lccn.loc.gov/2021063072

This book is printed on acid-free paper.

22 23 24 25 26 10 9 8 7 6 5 4 3 2 1

QUICK USE GUIDE

1. **Hope Makers:** *Trauma brain, society, and the power of you*

   Trauma, stress, and its impact on the brain. A close look at neural plasticity and how you are a game-changer for student healing, mental wellness, and hope.

2. **Healing:** *Safety, coping, and connections*

   Safety: *Trauma, safety, and fostering healing*

   The three Cs to create a safe healing environment.

   Coping: *Strategies and tools to help daily interactions*

   Three practical cognitive behavior strategies to help students cope and heal—**g**rounding, **a**nalyzing, and **p**rogress building (GAP).

   Connections: *Building positive relationships and repairing trust*

   Learn how to guide connection and reintegration using asset-based education to support relationships and positive connections.

   Compassion for Colleagues: *Building a healing culture of support*

3. **Overcoming:** *Hope and goals*

   Hope: *Using hope scores to foster resilience from setback, trauma, and ACEs*

   Learn to measure hope using the Children's Hope Scale and start cultivating hope with models, pathway flowcharts, and hopeful collaboration.

   Goals: *Using the learning goal cycle to build hope and success*

   Explore how goal stretching increases success and hope using the learning goal cycle to improve academic achievement.

   Compassion for Colleagues: *Growing hopeful cultures for the long game*

4. Planning: *Pathways, belief, and practicing*

Pathways: *Possibility blindness and learning*

Fostering productive struggle to support pathways using confidence boosters and utilizing the building new pathways tool to help student problem-solving.

Belief: *Using representation, social models, and environments to foster possibility*

Employ purposeful academic representation and social models through the creation of a wall of achievement or by showcasing diverse faces of success. Teach students to use the dreams-to-goal breakdown sheet to build belief and pathway possibilities.

Practicing: *Creating and using pathways for problems*

Help students prepare and plan for problems using the pathways milestones and problems-to-pathways activities to develop their ability to tackle goal barriers to increase their hope.

Compassion for Colleagues: *Pathways for problematic organizational practices and lack of support*

5. Energizing: *Agency and motivation*

Agency: *Building agency with willpower strategies*

Learn four key strategies to prevent burnout and support student willpower in times of trial and discover the keys to helping students form positive habits.

Motivation: *Infusing intrinsic drive and positive mindsets*

Utilize social supports and the built-in lesson engagement tool to meet students' psychological needs and simultaneously build intrinsic motvation.

Compassion for Colleagues: *Supporting and motivating each other*

6. The School of HOPE: *Patience, support, and connections for your journey*

Personal support and further resources for your journey to build hope, wellness, and fulfillment into daily education.

CONTENTS

For downloadable resources related to *The School of Hope*,
visit the companion website at
resources.corwin.com/TheSchoolofHope

ACKNOWLEDGMENTS

Hope happens in many ways, and these friends pushed, prodded, and believed in me, filling my cup and extending my hope. They supported this book becoming a book. For all they've done, I am truly grateful.

First, to my past, present, and future students, you are my *why* and I thank you for every moment.

Jessica Allan and Mia Rodriguez—I thought my GPS was great at guidance, but you're better! Great editing!

Shannon Kelly—May your red ink flow! Thank you for careful copy editing and for being a joy to work with.

Meredith Johnson—You push me to dive deeper in my writing and are always willing to read a chapter or two. For your honesty and enthusiasm, I thank you.

Helen Barrier—To the woman who gives me glows and grows and models loving feedback. I am blessed to know you.

Dr. Holly Deemer—You have been there as a professor, mentor, reader, and friend. Your support means the world to me!

Susan Morrison and Sandy Albertson, and the whole eighth-grade team at TMS—Thank you for your support and love.

Marynn Dause—You helped me learn to believe in myself and are always willing to take on crazy challenges with me. For the courage you give me, I thank you.

Brain Bicknell—Your artistic abilities put Picasso to shame. Thankful for your skills and how they enhance my writing!

Eileen Fitzsimmons and Carolyn Shaw—You are the best co-teachers of all time. That is all.

Patricia Davis—Thank you for being a sounding board. You're amazing!

Heather, Sandy, Angie, Ligia, Michelle, and Cathy—Thank you for your help and guidance throughout the process of writing this book.

Mom and my dearly departed father—Without you, I wouldn't exist! Thank you for raising me with hope.

C. J., Xander, Dominick, Sydney, Bella, Jacqueline, and Joseph—you made me a mom and it is my most cherished role.

Lastly, thank you to my rock in the storms of life, Matt. It's easy to have high hope with you by my side.

PUBLISHER'S ACKNOWLEDGMENTS

Corwin gratefully acknowledges the contributions of the following reviewers:

Carrie Jane Carpenter
ELA, SS, and reading educator
Educational Consultant,
   Oregon Teacher of the Year 2003
Redmond, Oregon

Jessica Johnson
Principal
Dodgeland School District
Juneau, WI

Susan Stone Kessler
Executive principal
Hunters Lane High School
Nashville, TN

Susan Kunz
School psychologist
Conejo Valley Unified School District
Thousand Oaks, CA

John F. Mahoney
Classroom mathematics teacher
Banneker Academic High School
Bethesda, MD

Debra Paradowski
Associate principal/administrator
Arrowhead Union High School
Hartland, WI

Melissa Pardue
Assistant principal
Pascagoula-Gautier School District
Pascagoula, MS

Ernie Rambo
Programs coordinator
Nevada National Board Professional
   Learning Institute
Las Vegas, NV

ABOUT THE AUTHOR

Cathleen Beachboard is a teacher, author, and researcher. She writes and creates content for Edutopia and has been featured by TED-Ed. After adopting five children out of a case of extreme abuse and neglect, she has been on a mission to improve outcomes for those who experience trauma and anxiety. Cathleen has taught middle school English for the past fifteen years. She also works as a part-time researcher holding an MA in psychology. Her research focuses on psychological tools schools can use to help students and staff increase psychological hope, resiliency, achievement, and happiness. You can find her on Twitter @Cathleenbeachbd.

ABOUT THE ILLUSTRATOR

Brian Bicknell is an illustrator and commercial artist. His work has appeared in media and publications both in the United States and internationally. Brian has collaborated on comics, graphic novels, television, commercials, and films. He has also served as a co-writer/illustrator for numerous publications.

Brian runs Bicknell Designs (bicknelldesigns.com) and uses art to inspire hope, action, and change. He currently resides with his wife and children on the North Shore of Massachusetts.

A NOTE FROM THE AUTHOR

Every story in this book is true. Names, personal characteristics, and settings have been changed to protect the privacy of my students and colleagues. Any resulting resemblance to other persons, living or dead, is coincidental and unintentional.

Trauma and stress can change your brain, but so can you with neural plasticity.
HAVE HOPE.
Goals
(WHAT POWER)
HOPE
Pathways
(WAY POWER)
Agency
(WILL POWER)

CHAPTER 1

HOPE MAKERS

People are born with hope. The moment your eyes open to this great big world, life takes hold. As young children, we seek to discover the world's secrets. We push ourselves to learn and master its wonders. Curiosity controls our days. Then it starts to become messy. Maybe, for you, it was when your cat ran away, or perhaps it hit you when a beloved family member died, or you felt it when you lost your best friend: pain. This is life too, after all, and this is hard.

Eventually, life is no longer simple. Some days are blue skies and others rain. On most days the clouds of sadness can be kept at bay, but sometimes they leak in and take the form of tears on your paper.

Will hope prevail? For one of my former students, it almost ran out.

I remember the moment vividly. It was a late Friday evening. I told my husband it would only be a few minutes until we could leave to go out, and he rolled his eyes. I just needed to write one quick school e-mail to start the weekend. I never wrote that e-mail. When I opened my inbox, a subject line stood out in bold. It merely said "bye." It was from a current student. Curious, I got sidetracked and opened the e-mail. It started with words that are forever etched in my brain: "I am completely broken." Various lines jumped out to me from the computer screen. I read with more worry and alarm. "I know you care, but no one wants to talk to me or help me. I just can't keep going on. People bully me and look at me weird. I feel so bad. I'm sorry. Goodbye."

I sat in shock for a minute, and then my brain went into action. I'd had no idea that this student was suffering. I felt overwhelmed, helpless, and desperate, all in one instant. Quickly I called the principal and school counselor for guidance. They took over. Phone calls were made. A crisis was averted, but it left me drained and empty.

How could I teach a kid every day, connect with that kid, and not once see this pain? Could this moment have been averted? School counselors and psychologists are equipped for these moments, but could I have provided tools and support for mental wellness in the classroom? The thoughts nagged at me.

School counselors and psychologists typically have hundreds to thousands of students on their caseload. The school counselor also didn't know about this moment until I did. She was running ragged, helping kids. There had to be something that could be done. Some intermediary that could help improve the well-being of the students and school staff.

How could the student have lost hope? In the question stood the answer: hope.

HOPE

We hear people use the term *hope* every day. But what exactly is it? People use it in daily conversations: "I hope I get this job." "I hope tomorrow's better." "I hope I win." The word *hope* has developed a vague definition. It intermixes wishful thinking and a bit of luck. It hints that something will take place magically, without effort. In this definition of *hope*, a passive bystander waits for an outcome to appear. Many people are unaware of the power behind this small four-letter word.

According to science, the hope you have inside and the hope mentioned in this book is an active force that plays a pivotal role in a person's life and future success. Psychological hope aids a person's cognition by providing goals, pathways, and agency to achieve outcomes. Dr. Charles R. Snyder, a psychologist and pioneer on hope research from the University of Kansas, says, "Hope is a positive cognitive state based on a sense of successful goal-directed determination and planning to meet these goals."[1] Hope is not an obscure concept with a vague definition; it is a powerful, scientifically quantifiable force that drives a person to positive life outcomes.

Hope has been proven to help a person achieve goals, increase positive life outcomes, aid in academic achievement and educational attainment, and contribute to a person's personal and psychological health. Even in the face of difficult life circumstances, hope allows a person to conceive of and aim for a different future. It is a powerful force. It gives a person a pathway to reach the potential they have inside. Hope helps us endure. Hope helps us thrive.

> Hope has been proven to help a person achieve goals, increase positive life outcomes, aid in academic achievement and educational attainment, and contribute to a person's personal and psychological health.

The studies on hope and its impact are numerous. Psychologists have researched how to test it, strengthen it, and nurture it. They've discovered that those with high hope scores tend to be more resilient and have higher life satisfaction levels regardless of family background, socioeconomic status, or adverse childhood experiences (ACEs). Hope is an equal opportunity asset all people can access. It's a powerful cognitive asset that could help schools improve academic achievement, motivate and assist our most vulnerable students, and provide a protective buffer against psychological stress and trauma.

So how is hope created? Three primary components work together to form hope: goals, agency, and pathways. Hope becomes a way of thinking that we utilize in every aspect of our life. It impacts whether we set easy or hard goals, if we can find ways to solve problems, and if we have the will to even try. Hope can be strengthened or weakened through various practices, relationships, and experiences. The people we interact with and the things we face teach us to hope or give up.

> Three primary components work together to form hope: goals, agency, and pathways.

FIGURE 1.1 HOPE

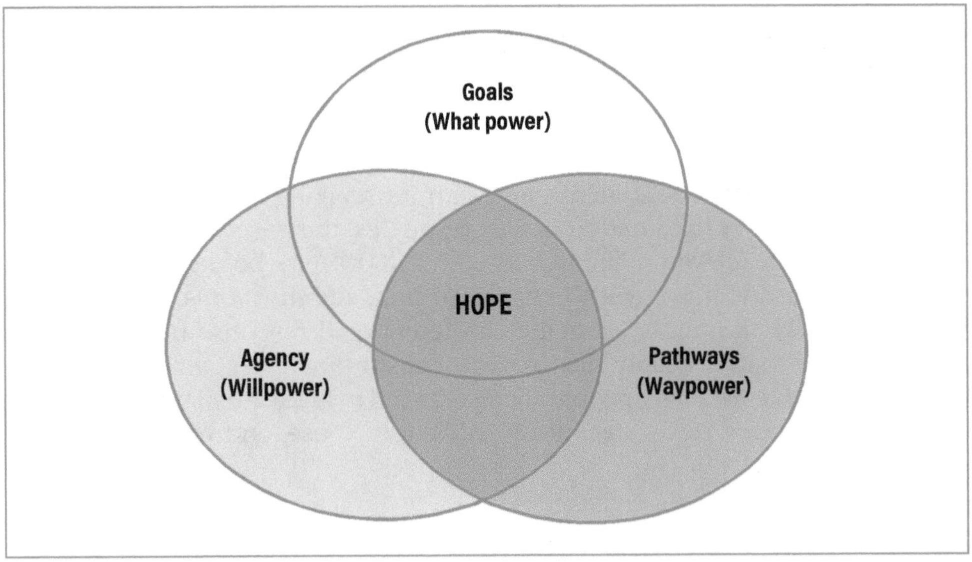

SOURCE: Adapted from Snyder, C. (2002). Hope theory: Rainbows in the mind. *Psychological Inquiry*, *13*(4), 249–275. http://jstor.org/stable/1448867

With so many positive results linked to it, we need to start interweaving psychological hope into school. People need hope because reality can be dark. Sometimes moments can get so dark that hope dims and fights to go on. My student faced a moment of darkness, and the reality is she isn't alone.

THE REALITY

According to health insurance data from forty-one million health records,[2] "Major depression is on the rise among Americans from all age groups but is rising fastest among teens and young adults." This statistic has a significant impact on hope because hope negatively correlates to depression. As one rises, the other falls. It seems the average person is losing hope. What could be causing this, and how can we stop it?

First, we need to look at neurobiology. Your brain has safety mechanisms to remember danger to keep you safe.[3] In the days of our early ancestors, remembering that you nearly drowned in a lake might make you walk a dryer, safer path. That trauma was a guidepost in your mind to keep destruction away. Remembering and reliving minor pain kept you in balance. It wasn't around all the time and served a purpose.

Fast forward to today. That same brain that remembers pain and reacts with fight, flight, or freeze is thrown into modern society, constantly connected to the happenings of the world. The news and Internet broadcast famine, destruction, and pain. Broadcasters choose to show the tragedies. Fire down the street? Buy an extinguisher. Robbery down the road? Lock your doors. The world is doing you a service by highlighting everyday problems. You see the pain and therefore avoid it. However, how can you avoid it if it's everywhere? What if that same lake that nearly drowned your early ancestor surrounded him? He had to see it every day, every second, and out of nowhere, the lake would pop back up. What would happen?

Every day more teachers, students, and staff are walking into school buildings with larger problems. In a nation of vast resources, thirty-seven million people are going hungry (eleven million children),[4] 553,000 are homeless,[5] and more than 10 percent lives in poverty.[6] On top of that, add in trauma. According to *Psychology Today,* trauma is defined as an "emotional response to an event or an experience that is deeply distressing or disturbing."[7] So, while witnessing the world's problems, many people are also forced to face everyday traumas that can befall them due to divorce, death, addiction, abuse, and neglect, to name some sources.

> Trauma is defined as an "emotional response to an event or an experience that is deeply distressing or disturbing."

To protect us, our brains and bodies are built to adapt to trauma and change. Over a short period, those adaptations might be helpful to get a person through a tough moment. However, those adaptations can negatively impact a person's quality of life and health over the long term. Various forms of physical and emotional abuse, neglect, and household dysfunction that occur before age eighteen are classified as ACEs. The category was later expanded beyond the original scale to include forms of oppression and environmental determinants of health. The Centers for Disease Control and Prevention (CDC) discovered a direct link between ACEs and risky health behaviors, chronic health conditions, low life potential, and early death. ACEs are common among people.[8] According to the National Survey of Children's Health (NSCH) in 2018, "Almost half of the nation's children have experienced one or more types of serious childhood trauma."[9] So, in an average class of twenty-eight kids, fourteen of them have experienced trauma. It's not just *some* kids who experience trauma, *it's most* kids.

According to the National Survey of Children's Health (NSCH) in 2018, "Almost half of the nation's children have experienced one or more types of serious childhood trauma."

That average can increase drastically with natural disasters, environmental factors, and global catastrophes. For example, the global pandemic of COVID-19 has caused more children to experience trauma due to families losing jobs and income, quarantining and isolation, and a fear of leaving home due to the threat of illness. As the number of ACEs increases, so does the risk for negative life repercussions. The biggest problem is that if a person's mental health isn't addressed, the toxic stress that develops from ACEs can change the human brain.

The global pandemic of COVID-19 has caused more children to experience trauma due to families losing jobs and income, quarantining and isolation, and a fear of leaving home due to the threat of illness.

The human brain is highly malleable. It adapts and changes as a result of our interactions with our environment. Neuroplasticity starts when our brain begins to develop; cells come together and reorganize in response to the body's changing needs. The brain continues adapting and evolving through our entire lives until the day we die.[10] Neuroplasticity is the reason the early ancestor from above, who nearly drowned in the lake, developed an aversion to water. His brain adapted and created pathways to fear water.

Neuroplasticity is also a reason to have hope. The brain can adapt and change to new positive stimuli just as readily as it adapts to negative stimuli. The man with the fear of water can also conquer that fear. Our brains are not set in stone. There is hope that the brain can overcome past traumatic events that evoke anxiety and stress. However, it won't be easy. Having stress pathways in the brain constantly on high alert from trauma leads to anxiety and impaired learning and memory. Your brain adapts to prolonged trauma with decreased gray matter in the prefrontal cortex and increased amygdala volume to make you hypervigilant, which reduces attention control.[11] Basically, a person who is used to being unsafe is continuously on the lookout for the next hazardous moment. A person can't concentrate on learning when perpetually on the lookout for pain.

That overwhelming feeling is similar to getting struck by a wave in the ocean. It sucks you under, but you push to the surface, catch your breath, and adapt. A wave in the sea isn't so bad until it becomes wave after wave after wave. Teachers must gain practices to help relieve trauma so they can free students to concentrate and grow. If a teacher's job is to help students learn, it's vital to recognize that trauma can hinder learning during even the greatest lesson.

> Teachers must gain practices to help relieve trauma so they can free students to concentrate and grow.

Sometimes we want to dive in to rescue those we see in pain. Caregivers of people in trauma have the potential to develop vicarious trauma or compassion fatigue from trying to help those stuck in the deep waters of despair. You jump in to save someone but wind up stuck and need to save yourself. You try to help, but while pouring out compassion for the trauma of children, co-workers, or staff, you can become drained and overwhelmed. It can even cause you to feel depressed. You cannot pour from an empty cup, but you keep trying.

Most of us have learned to insulate ourselves against the hurts of the world. This armor is for protection. It keeps the pain away and our feelings in check. It's better to feel nothing than be overwhelmed, right? It keeps the world out. When we feel weak, we go to our armor for strength. Pain bounces off the armor like rain hitting a windshield. It puts a barrier between knowing a person and caring for them. We choose to save ourselves because there seems to be no other way.

Armor creates a divide. It's great for protecting feelings, but those with trauma don't have the luxury of turning their back on what they've experienced. Surrounded by trauma, they feel and react. They don't have the privilege of choosing to look away. We offer armor as a coping mechanism, but full protection does not exist. People who experience trauma can't protect themselves from their reality. The sad thing is choosing to look away from the pain causes us to miss something important—genuinely seeing and understanding a person.

The good news is there is a key to countering trauma: hope. Hope is not a fixed quantity, and with a mix of positive psychology, social-emotional learning (SEL), and trauma-informed practices, we can provide it to others. We can shed our armor, balance our cup of caring, and do more with what we have. We have the ability to change the world. We have the ability to help. We can create school cultures and classrooms of hope. And it starts with you.

> Hope is not a fixed quantity, and with a mix of positive psychology, social-emotional learning (SEL), and trauma-informed practices, we can provide it to others.

WHY HOPE?

Hope gives us something to live for. It's necessary for dealing with problems and failures and gives us motivation to keep going in the face of obstacles. It helps us get back up when we get knocked down. The smallest seed of hope can keep us moving even in the darkest situation. The belief that a brighter moment exists right around the corner edges us just to keep going. Hope creates resilience.

Resilience has been documented in fMRI studies of the brain. Hope can be seen and felt. A neuroimaging research study on adolescent brains from 2017 revealed hope exists and impacts the medial orbitofrontal cortex. The medial orbitofrontal cortex is where our reward-related processing, motivation production, problem-solving, and goal-directed behaviors live. It's where we learn, grow, and plan for our future. The researchers discovered that as hope goes up, the neural activity associated with anxiety goes down.

> A neuroimaging research study on adolescent brains from 2017 revealed hope exists and impacts the medial orbitofrontal cortex.

FIGURE 1.2   HOPE IN THE BRAIN

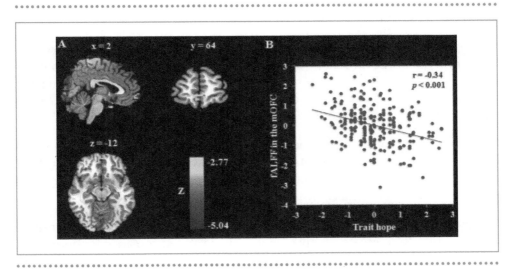

SOURCE: Wang, S., Xu, X., Zhou, M., Chen, T., Yang, X., Chen, G., & Gong, Q. (2017). Hope and the brain: Trait hope mediates the protective role of medial orbitofrontal cortex spontaneous activity against anxiety. *NeuroImage, 157*, 439–447. http://dx.doi.org.ezproxy.liberty.edu/10.1016/j.neuroimage.2017.05.056

What Does This Mean?

Hope can't take away the pain or fix your problems, but these results show hope works to help us think critically and keep going despite the anxiety or stress we face. Hope helps us bounce back, supporting the brain to form new neural pathways and learn new ways of thinking even amid difficulties. The brain can do its job and think so we can do our jobs and teach.

Hope fosters resilience, which helps students face problems and bounce back throughout their lives. Hope breeds happier, more successful, and healthier people who can face adversity and overcome it. Our children deserve success, happiness, and overall wellness. Hope starts with positive attachments. The relationships you build make all the difference in the world.

> Hope fosters resilience, which helps students face problems and bounce back throughout their lives. Hope breeds happier, more successful, and healthier people who can face adversity and overcome it.

ISOLATION AND ATTACHMENT

Relationships matter more today than ever because the modern world can be very isolating. You can go through an entire day and never speak to a person. Need to talk to a friend? Send a text. Need groceries? Get them delivered to your door. Need to work on a project with a group? Meet on Google and work on the document at the same time. We can connect instantly but go through the whole day without one human touch, spoken word, or smile.

Through screens and filters, people don't always notice the tear in the corner of a person's eye or the face that winces in pain. Even if they do, they may ignore it because it's hard to look suffering in the face. It's one of the reasons we run from vulnerability. Pain. Is. Hard. We may look at each other, but we don't *see* each other. You can change that.

School is one of the few places people still have the chance to connect. You can show people they matter. Students and staff cannot do effective work if they don't feel safe, known, and cared for within their schools. We can give compassion and provide meaningful connections.

When you take the time to gain tools to interact and connect, it matters. Positive school connections create positive school culture. When you are intentional with meeting people where they are, you give them a chance to grow.

> Positive school connections create positive school culture.

I got into education to make a difference and inspire others to greatness. That starts with hope. Today more than ever, people need hope. Through the strategies, tools, and resources provided in this book, you will gain new ways to foster hope and lead people to a more positive outlook.

CONNECTIONS OF HOPE

Why does a positive outlook matter? Because our views either become ladders to more extraordinary things or walls of limitation. When people go through pain or trauma, they build walls, which don't allow others in and keep a person isolated from the world, much like armor. It's a natural human reaction. The early man who nearly drowned in the water built a wall to avoid all things wet. He did this to protect himself from getting hurt again. A wall of fear hinders him from seeing the good side of water. He no longer trusts water. Avoiding the water keeps him safe but limits him from leading a full life.

> When people go through pain or trauma, they build walls, which don't allow others in and keep a person isolated from the world, much like armor.

People who have experienced trauma lower their trust in the world.[12] A person who lacks trust is going to have trouble building relationships and facing fears. By following a path of trauma-informed practices centered around building hope that we will explore in the following chapters, you will gain a map of understanding to dismantle barriers of fear. With the help of a trusted person, the early man might have had the courage to walk near the water. Perhaps he would even have had the gusto to learn to swim. Providing that bond can give someone a chance to envision a brighter future.

The most exciting news? The relationships you form and the practices you employ can change the weighted impact of trauma.[13] Imagine a two-sided scale with trauma on one side and relationships, hope, resiliency, and coping skills on the other side. As we fill up the positive side of the scale, the weight of trauma becomes less. That's why two people can go through the same traumatic situation and have entirely different reactions. It all depends on how much positive weight a person has when trauma occurs. As educators, we can help change the impact trauma has on others and provide a shield of hope to help others push through difficult times. The relationships we provide can go beyond nurturing and supportive, they can be transformative.

The people who are going to change the world don't need to be presidents, members of the United Nations, or diplomats. It can start simply with us, one person at a time. Let's start this journey of possibilities together. Together we can create a movement to put well-being in front of test scores, caring in front of curriculum, and show the world the most important lesson: that we exist to help and care for each other.

> Together we can create a movement to put well-being in front of test scores, caring in front of curriculum, and show the world the most important lesson: that we exist to help and care for each other.

This book is organized into four sections that break down resources to help schools foster hope. The four main sections spell out HOPE to make them easy to remember (healing, overcoming, planning, and energizing).

Section one, "Healing," contains ways to help people with hurts and trauma. Section two, "Overcoming," deals with resources and tools used in positive psychology to support budding hope and counteract maladaptive thinking processes that hold a person back. The third section, "Planning," deals with fostering resiliency through practices that develop problem-solving skills and ways to face trials and problems. The last section, "Energizing," focuses on tools to grow internal motivation and a person's drive to succeed. Every chapter ends with a "Compassion for Colleagues" section that addresses how to use tools presented in the chapter to support staff members and foster school cultures of hope.

Througout the chapters I have added section stops to allow you to process information and develop ways to apply what you learn. My hope is that you continue your thinking with colleagues, both in person and online (using the hashtag #HOPEforEdu). Your voice, thoughts, and ideas are essential in this discussion. We can create lasting change because none of us can do what all of us can do. It is not enough for a single educator to nurture hope in our students. We need to build entire school communities that work together to ensure all students thrive and utilize hope to promote purpose and self-worth. This should be done not only for the children, but also for the teachers, service providers, and administrators who serve them. A school of hope.

As Aristotle once said, "Educating the mind without educating the heart is no education at all."

 **HEART TO HEART**

QUESTIONS AND IDEAS FOR ACTION

Reflect, discuss with a group, or share your thoughts on social media using the book's hashtag, #HOPEforEdu.

Questions

1. How does the rise in depression for teens and young adults relate to anything you have discovered or noticed in your own profession, organization, or community?

2. What do the findings on how ACEs and trauma impact the brain mean to your profession, organization, or community? How does this information impact the day-to-day in the classroom?

3. Relationships can change the weighted impact of trauma. Give an example from your own life when a relationship truly helped you or someone you know through a tough moment or traumatic event. How did that relationship impact the person?

4. It's hard to justify working on mental wellness in school because it's not part of the curriculum. How would you defend using time, energy, and school resources to increase mental wellness for students and staff?

Ideas for Action

- Be intentional and expose yourself to the needs, problems, strengths, and assets in your community. The community is the backbone of every school. Getting to know the weaknesses, strengths, and people who make up the community gives you insight into the backstories of students and staff.

- Schedule time to talk with someone you feel is making a positive difference in the well-being of others. Ask them what keeps them going on tough days. What tools do they use? How do they help others when they are experiencing trauma?

- There are numerous stories of how a teacher sparked hope and transformation for a student despite the challenges the student was facing. Either recall an instance from your career in education where you spurred hope and transformation for a student or look up a story where another teacher made a difference. What did you or the teacher in the story do that helped students flourish?

CHAPTER 2

HEALING

Tears ran down Jordan's cheeks as she sat writing in her journal. I asked her if she wanted to talk. Nodding, she followed me to the doorway. Once outside, she told me her father might be going back to jail. She sobbed as she wondered aloud where she would go. Jordan's story turned into the tale of a mother who was out of the picture and a family that rejected her. I hugged her. The weight of the world was on her shoulders. "I care for you, and so do a lot of other people. What you're going through isn't easy, but you'll get through this, Jordan. For now, take a breath and look at what you know. Just take it moment by moment."

A few days later, Sean tells me he is haunted from finding the dead body of a friend on his couch. It echoes in his head. Aaron whispers to me that his mom and her boyfriend broke up. He knows his mom doesn't have money to pay the rent. Every day he worries they will lose everything.

The walls of the school stand firm as the foundations of people within them tremble. I sit with them. I listen. I give them a safe space. You can't skip to hope from despair. The path to hope starts with safety because trauma is anything but safe.

You don't usually see trauma coming. You fall into it much like a pit. Maybe yours came because of a disease, the loss of someone you cared about, or pain caused by another. The first thing you feel is pain as you hit the bottom. This is followed by a desperate attempt to get out of the pit. Your only quest is to escape from the deep feelings, avoid more pain, and search for safety. After so many days, the pit can become a grave for hope. And that's precisely what happened to my own children.

ENTER PAIN

My world, life views, and purpose changed the day my five children arrived on my doorstep. My husband and I had trained for weeks to get to this point. We watched videos explaining trauma, read books on relationships, trained in mental health first aid, and took classes to learn parenting techniques. According to the Department of Social Services, we were certified, well-rounded parents. According to the world, we had all the preparation we needed. We both wanted nothing more than to be a loving mom and dad.

Then the kids showed up, and despite the books, training, classroom experiences, and parenting groups, nothing had prepared me. Their problems weren't black-and-white case studies. I wanted nothing more than to love them and see them happy.

Sadly, my five children had come from a situation that was anything but happy. The police report, written by a veteran officer, stated that when he had picked them up, their home was filled with rotten food and mountains of trash bags infested with flies, maggots, and gnats. He stated that it was one of the worst situations he had ever witnessed in all his years as a police officer.

The children had been neglected and abused at the hands of their parents. The adults who were supposed to shelter and protect them had betrayed them. After they were removed from their home, they were bounced round to a few foster families. At night Dominick, one of my younger boys, would cry and shake as a mechanism to fall asleep. He wrapped himself in trauma instead of blankets. Their world had been shattered. They had come to live in the pit of trauma. Hope was a distant memory.

The moment they crossed the threshold I swore to myself that I would help bring them out of the pit. I knew the odds were stacked against me. My children had enough adverse childhood experiences (ACEs) to fill two hands, and they were all under ten. I wanted to see them happy, but I was in for a fight because the brain doesn't want to let go of pain.

Trauma sticks with us. We tend to define ourselves according to our catastrophes. As I stated in the first chapter, the human brain remembers trauma clearly to keep you safe. A research study published in the Association for Psychological Science by Boston College psychologist Elizabeth Kensinger shows "that whether an event is pleasurable or aversive seems to be a critical determinant of the accuracy with which the event is remembered, with negative events being remembered in greater detail than positive ones."[1] It's the reason you might not recall what happened in February 2020 but most likely remember March of 2020 when COVID-19 impacted schools and states everywhere. The brain recalls dangerous moments to help us isolate what caused us danger. It's the reason some people can remember great details of situations and others choose to repress the moment.

Helping create a safe environment for students that fosters healing allows the brain to concentrate on learning. The purpose of school and teaching is to educate students, and we can't do that properly if we don't help students with trauma. It's imperative for schools to create school cultures that recognize, understand, and implement practices to help a student access the curriculum. Having resources that help all students feel safe is essential for enhancing children's cognitive capacity and inspiring them to learn. Plus, these healing-centered practices can challenge views students may have of themselves, their relationships with adults, and even their life circumstances. If we want to truly teach students, we have to provide a place where students feel protected so they can heal and learn.

RECOGNIZING TRAUMA

No matter how hard I wanted to cover up or erase the pain my children experienced, I couldn't. We can't change what's already been done. I couldn't change Jordan's situation. I couldn't wave a wand and make her problems within her family dissipate. School doors welcome all kinds of people who carry all kinds of burdens. What do all the people walking into your building need? To feel safe. For most, feeling safe will come easily with a simple welcoming smile, but for those who have trauma or ACEs, it's not so easy.

When you fall into the pit of trauma, the first thing you worry about is the environment. Will you get hurt more? Will the ground give way? Will you start falling again? You want safety, but trauma has broken your trust. When my children arrived, I showed them their rooms and where to store their belongings, set some ground rules, and went straight to relationship building. That's the first mistake I made. My children had been forcibly controlled for their entire lives, and I unknowingly triggered a trauma response by giving them very little sense of control. They saw their rooms and new belongings but immediately ran to huddle together in the living room.

I didn't understand. Everything looked safe but didn't feel safe. It also hit me that they would have to go to school with this pain and these survival reactions. What would happen to them there? Would they be lost in the crowd? Would they suffer in silence? Their situation made me wonder how many people go to school with invisible backpacks full of pain.

It's necessary to know that children with trauma may take longer to feel safe because their brains have dug out a neural pathway of survival reactions to keep them safe. A person's thoughts and feelings are similar to water flowing on a surface. The more a person's thoughts run in one direction, the deeper the folds of a neural pathway become. New thoughts want to adhere to the carved pathway because it's the easiest way to go. The pathway didn't form overnight, and that's great news because it gives educators a formula to follow to help kids form new neural pathways. With time, safe environmental stimuli, and reinforcement we can help children form new, positive pathways. Neuroplasticity shows that the brain can adapt and change. With the right tools, we can help students learn they can move from surviving to thriving. We just need to differentiate safety needs the same way we differentiate instruction—by identifying students who may require more scaffolding to feel safe.

It's important to take the time to look for trauma. It's also important to note that there are varying degrees of trauma, from ACEs to acute traumas that stem from a negative event such as a sickness. Regardless of the degree of trauma, *all* trauma affects the brain. Figure 2.1 provides a list of some of the ways trauma presents in a child. For example, one child might show trauma through behavior or impulse control, whereas another child's trauma might manifest through distrust and not forming supportive relationships. It's important to remember that not all kids will show all these signs; some will show very few, and some will show no signs at all.

It's also important to note that having signs of possible trauma does not mean trauma has occurred. It's not up to teachers to diagnose trauma but to be aware of how to work with kids who may present signs indicating trauma. The goal is for us as teachers to create an environment that fosters healing so students can grow and thrive.

The most important healing tool at our disposal is ... us. You and me. We can offer one of the strongest and most long-lasting protective factors for a student: a positive relationship. Once a student trusts in the safety of the classroom they will begin to reach out, and it's our job to be there when they do. Positive relationships have the power to expedite healing and can diminish the long-term mental and health impacts of trauma.[2] Plus, building a relationship that helps a student enjoy school can help a student remain resilient, even during traumatic experiences.[3] The connections we build are a game-changer for fostering healing.

> Positive relationships have the power to expedite healing and can diminish the long-term mental and health impacts of trauma.

It's important to note that forming relationships with those who have experienced trauma isn't easy. Once a teacher becomes a "safe relationship" they will at times bear the brunt of anger, mixed emotions, and mistrust from the traumatized person as that person processes emotions and situations to heal. It's easy to see reactions and behaviors in a negative light, but it's important to not devalue response skills a person has learned to survive. In some parts of their life, certain behaviors and skills may have kept this student alive. We need to honor rather than judge that. That's why it's imperative educators take an asset-based approach with behaviors, discipline, and relationships.[4]

SAFETY FIRST

Creating a safe environment is like lowering a first aid kit into the pit of trauma. It won't fix the pain from the fall, but it's a start to healing and hope.[5] It's tempting to jump in the pit and help from within, sidestepping safety to form a bond. Helping someone in pain by joining them in their pit helps *no one*. I made this mistake by trying immediately to form a bond with my children over commonalities and to make connections. My teacher's brain told me relationships should come first. It's what good teachers do. I asked them about their interests, but they refused to talk. I tried to play games and they would sit and stare at me. I would

FIGURE 2.1   WARNING SIGNS OF TRAUMA

WARNING SIGNS OF POSSIBLE TRAUMA

Attachments and Relationships

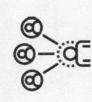

- Relationship problems with family, adults, and peers
- Problems with attachment and separation from caregivers
- Distrust
- Social isolation
- Difficulty relating to others perspectives

Physical Health: Body & Brain

- Sensory motor development problems
- Developmental delays/regressive behavior
- Trouble concentrating
- Inability to feel pain
- Somatization-production of recurrent medical symptoms with no discernible natural cause

Emotional Responses

- Difficulty with emotional self-regulation
- Difficulty labeling and expressing feelings
- Problems knowing and describing internal states
- Difficulty communicating wishes and needs
- Internalizing symptoms such as anxiety, depression, etc.

Dissociation

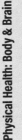

- Disconnection between thoughts, emotions, and/or perceptions
- Memory lapses/loss of orientation of place or time
- Depersonalization — a sense of not being in "one's body"
- Derealization — a sense that experiences are not real

Self Concept & Future Orientation

- Negative body image
- Low self-esteem
- Shame and guilt
- Negative expectations of the future or foreshortened sense of future

Thinking and Learning

- Difficulty with executive function and attention
- Lack of sustained curiosity
- Problems with information processing
- Problems focusing on and completing tasks
- Difficulties with planning and problem solving
- Negative self-talk

Behavior

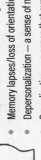

- Difficulties with impulse control
- Risk-taking behaviors
- Sleep disturbances
- Eating disturbances
- Oppositional behavior/difficulty with rules

SOURCE: Adapted from Cook, A., Spinazzola, J., Ford, J., Lanktree, C., Blaustein, M., Cloitre, M., DeRosa, R., Hubbard, R., Kagan, R., Liautaud, J., Mallah, K., Olafson, E., & Van der Kolk, B. (2005). Complex trauma in children and adolescents. *Psychiatric Annals, 35*(5), 390–398. https://doi.org/10.3928/00485713-20050501-05

do a normal activity like turn on the television and one would yell or cry. The more I tried to move closer the more they pushed away. You see, relationships are critical, but I forgot the importance of creating safety first. Developing connections in a relationship begins with building a framework of security. Establishing that an environment is safe allows a person to comfortably open up on their own terms and form attachments. A better bond forms when you give the child the chance to drive the bonding process.

Now take those same behaviors and throw them into a classroom of twenty-five students. You ask a question. A student refuses to respond. You attempt to engage them in a lesson and they stare or yell. You attempt to bond as they push you away. I was lucky enough to know my children had a backstory. What if you didn't know? The challenging behaviors of many traumatized people tend to result in controlling and even punitive responses from those who care for them. This storming stage is normal as a traumatized child tries to locate boundaries and test the waters for safety, but instead of being helped in their search for consistency, the kid is written up for defiance and gets labeled a troublemaker.

The reality is we've all used labels. We stick them on jars and file folders to know what's inside, and we stick them on people for the same reason. We point to a kid and label them a behavior problem or a trauma kid. End of discussion. So why do schools do this? Schools use labels to make sure everyone understands what's inside. It's efficient. Schools want to help everyone understand what's going on. Ultimately it's easier to talk about a person than it is to help them. It's easier to discuss a behavior than to address the underlying cause.

If we don't create environments founded on healing we're going to end up doing the same work repeatedly with students and getting the same outcomes. The labels become grave markers for growth. We need to provide a foundational healing environment that allows every person the opportunity to grow and thrive, and that starts with safety.

> We need to provide a foundational healing environment that allows every person the opportunity to grow and thrive, and that starts with safety.

CREATING SAFETY AND THE THREE CS: CONSISTENCY, COMMUNICATION, AND CARE

To create safety for students we need to make a valiant attempt to listen and respond to the thoughts of every person in our care.[6] When my children arrived, I wanted to have a relationship from the moment they walked in the door. I was unaware of stimuli in the environment that would trigger instability.

The quick way to alleviate possible stressors is to make sure every person has the opportunity to express their needs and concerns as routines, rules, and procedures are developed.

Consistency: Rules, Procedures, and Routines

Routines and norms offer consistency, which conveys safety and stability. It provides predictability that lets us know what's going to happen and when. When going over rules, routines, and procedures, consider allowing people to ask questions and give input in their creation.

As much as possible, co-creating classroom norms allows all students, including those who have experienced trauma, to have a voice in shaping a space that fosters a sense of safety. Creating rules, routines, and procedures with others provides a sense of security, value, and ownership, which enhances personal safety. It gives the person who might have experienced trauma the chance to bring up concerns and helps avoid recreating triggering situations where students felt like they weren't in control. It can stop potential problems from happening.

Co-creating classroom norms allows all students, including those who have experienced trauma, to have a voice in shaping a space that fosters a sense of safety.

This safety practice also begins to foster psychological hope in the brain. Setting a collaborative goal gives students ownership of their environment. The class works together daily to achieve the principles set in their goal. Students get to experience how this collaborative goal works to shape the classroom culture. This reinforces the power of setting goals and future planning. This practice shows students they have power to shape and change the world around them and builds hope as students see how their efforts impact the goal principles and classroom culture.

I like to start off the year by having students agree on the community principles they want to use as a goal to create their ideal classroom environment. Students give input on what attributes should form the foundation for classroom interactions. To get them started I provide them with examples by asking questions. Should we be able to trust each other in the classroom? What is necessary to keep you engaged, happy, and safe? From their individual lists, we create a large list of principles on the board. The students then group similar characteristics until we come up with a list of four or five attributes for the classroom.

Classroom ideals might include trustworthiness, humor, collaboration, and kindness. The class then works together to create one rule that will ensure that each of these ideals is honored. For example, trustworthiness might have a rule that we honor each other by being honest even when it's hard. Humor might have a rule that states we use school-appropriate jokes or puns when suitable to make class lighthearted. Collaboration might have a rule that we work together as a class to accomplish goals and to build comradery. Lastly, kindness could have a rule that states we always try to make others feel welcome by acting in a way that shows respect and caring. This allows students to see that the rules work to form a pathway to the goal of keeping them safe, comfortable, and happy.

Once the rules are created, I print out the principles and rules and give a copy to each member of the class. Each of my six classes creates principles and rules they will follow. It's important to go over rules and procedures often to remind people of the way to act in certain situations, to show the structures of consistency that are in place, and to convey to students and staff that safety is a priority.

We can't mitigate all stressors, but students are more likely to demonstrate resilience if they know they have a say and the support of a consistent, caring teacher. Even with a good foundation, however, problems may arise. The best thing we can do in any situation is reaffirm safety and take the time to be curious about behaviors. When students do exhibit challenging behaviors, we can reaffirm safety by approaching them in a calm, respectful way. Rather than asking, "What's wrong with you?" and labeling a kid, we should remain curious and shift the question to, "What's happened to you?"

> The best thing we can do in any situation is reaffirm safety and take the time to be curious about behaviors.

My own children kept huddling together in my home. Instead of becoming full of frustration, I asked them questions about the huddling behavior. My oldest son, C. J., later told me that huddle-hugging made them feel safe. I continued asking questions and found out they would group together to prevent severe injury. In the past, their father would isolate one of them to abuse, and they knew if they ran and hugged each other he might still hurt them, but not as much as if they were alone. They shared the pain. My children found safety in the clinging hands of their siblings, so when they arrived at my house they clung to each other not to snub their new life but because they wanted safety. This learned behavior was a way to self-soothe and find security during a gigantic change.

Change is hard, but it's even more difficult for those with trauma.[7] Even though my children were in a safe environment, their brains and bodies did not recognize that there was no danger. Consistency over time helps soothe the brain and gives comfort. After a few weeks of following the same routine, listening to my kids, and setting principles for the household environment, my children started to smile, play, and laugh. Your consistent words and actions matter beyond measure!

Communication: Mental Health Check-In

How do you handle your bad days, when hope is a distant star and "Happy" is just a song blaring from a radio? When you are exhausted, stressed, and just don't want to try?

You might play video games or read a book. Perhaps you distract yourself with the Internet, YouTube, or Netflix. A jog in the park might make you feel better. We have ways to cope, but do they solve the problem? They numb the pain, but do they remove it?

Coping mechanisms might get you through a tough spot, but it takes more to help foster healing. According to a study done by Pennebaker, Kiecolt-Glaser, and Glaser, "Simply talking about our problems and sharing our negative emotions with someone we trust can be profoundly healing—reducing stress, strengthening our immune system, and reducing physical and emotional distress."[8]

We need to talk more about mental well-being because a lack of communication will block us and stop us from forming connections. Communication helps people deal, heal, and cope with hurts. It also allows us to show students new ways to channel their feelings.

According to a study done by Pennebaker, Kiecolt-Glaser, and Glaser, "Simply talking about our problems and sharing our negative emotions with someone we trust can be profoundly healing—reducing stress, strengthening our immune system, and reducing physical and emotional distress."

It's important to have numerous opportunities for every person to check in and communicate their mental state. Each chance creates a net to catch, respond to, and assist in healing hurts as they arise. Mental health communication can be done in numerous ways in the classroom and school setting. Teachers can create spaces physically or remotely where every student can check in. Communication allows teachers to gain insight into student safety concerns, feedback, and traumas.

FIGURE 2.2   MENTAL HEALTH CHECK-IN FORM

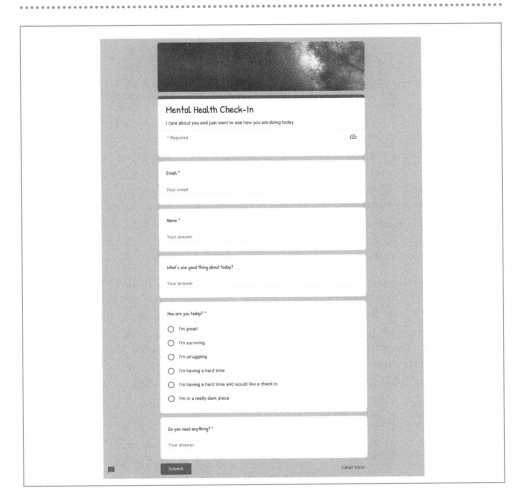

Consider creating a check-in using a Google Form that asks first about a positive part of a student's day. Then inquire specifically about the student's mental state. Using multiple-choice answers can help students feel less intimidated to complete the check-in. Offer choices such as "I'm great," "I'm OK," "I'm struggling," or "I'm having a hard time and would like a check-in." For younger students, consider using happy/sad faces that show varying degrees of emotion from happy to upset. Use an open-ended question to ask if the student has particular needs that can be addressed. You can make a copy of the Google Form I use with my students (displayed on the previous page) by going to https://forms.gle/QTxXSNn4Lr9fqQ2H8. Pass out the link, post it in a digital classroom, or create a QR code for students to scan to allow easy access. Provide a few minutes for students to fill out the chart at the start of class. Quickly scan the results for any people in need of a physical check-in and follow up.

The greatest thing of value in a school is the people. Taking the time to check in and help others shows people that they matter. It allows safety to bloom and alleviates fear. Having open conversations about mental health promotes a school culture of mental wellness. Trauma can touch anyone at any time, but with open communication we can be there when it does.

Having open conversations about mental health promotes a school culture of mental wellness.

Care: Self-Care Plans and Asset-Based Teaching

When trauma shows up it arrives like an earthquake, which can wreck consistency. Even when it stops, aftershocks occur. Stressful moments are the breeding place of rash decisions. Why? Because without proper planning, we react to the moment. The reality is that over time acute traumas touch all of us: death, sickness, accidents, divorce, and natural disasters, to name a few. Schools prepare and run drills for shootings, fires, and tornados. In California, they even build schools with the knowledge that earthquakes may happen. Addressing mental wellness is just as important as preparing for a fire. It's important to have tools at our disposal to provide care for those we serve. In order to do that, we need to plan for bad days and moments of emotional turmoil.[9]

A self-care plan is an intervention that keeps a person from being completely sucked into an emotional reaction. It can give a sense of control and safety during escalating feelings. Having a self-care plan is like earthquake-proofing a building. It won't stop the earthquake when it hits, but it will give a person a choice in how to respond. Each person creates his or her own self-care plan. It's a preventative measure filled with their favorite self-care activities, self-regulation tools, and ideas for how to utilize the people who support them.

A self-care plan is an intervention that keeps a person from being completely sucked into an emotional reaction. It can give a sense of control and safety during escalating feelings.

Having a plan takes the guesswork out of what to do and where to turn in a moment of crisis. It helps a person respond instead of react to the situation at hand. It allows them to take time to think about what they want to do and how they want to do it. You can write your own self-care plan and get students to do the same. Having students create individual plans gives teachers tools to support students who show signs of distress and provides teachers with strategies, activities, and tools to help each student.

For example, Jordan struggled with feelings about her dad going back to prison. In her plan, she wrote that her dad being in and out of her life was a stressor and sometimes caused her to shut down. I knew from her self-care plan that I was an adult she relied on and that art was a tool she used to feel better, so after she finished talking, I suggested she take a few minutes to draw when she went back to the classroom. By taking those few minutes, she was able to find a safe space to deal with her feelings. Creating plans with students allows them to utilize their own neuroplasticity to reshape a moment of chaos into one of control.

> Creating plans with students allows them to utilize their own neuroplasticity to reshape a moment of chaos into one of control.

To begin a self-care plan with a student, have them recognize support structures, people, and hobbies that help them feel better. Start by asking the student to list activities that they currently utilize to help them feel calm or happy. It's best to model an example plan to students as they create their own. I have each of my students fill out this Google Doc when they are creating their plan: https://rb.gy/lcie3x

To model, I go through the self-care plan and fill one out for myself. I go through it step by step and explain out loud my thought process for each part. For calming activities, I give students suggestions of activities such as music, exercise, coloring, art, meditation, etc. Next, I have them list one or two people whom they can turn to for help and support. In the same section, they should write down what resources they have access to in the school building. For example, if your school has a school counselor or a focus and recovery (FAR) room, students can utilize those. By writing this list, the student can take mental stock of tools at their disposal in times of turmoil.

Once students complete the support section, they should list stressors or things that might act as a speedbump to their mental well-being. This section will serve as a guide for moments when you might utilize a student's self-care plan. Thinking through a typical school day or school year might help them hone in on specific areas of stress, such as transitions between classes, a specific time of year, or perhaps a situation like a fire drill. Then they should list barriers outside of school that might affect their mental well-being. Lastly, they should create a plan to address each of the stressors and barriers. They can use tools from their feel-good activity list or other strategies they might

FIGURE 2.3   MY DAILY SELF-CARE PLAN

MY DAILY SELF-CARE PLAN

BODY	MIND	SOCIAL	EMOTIONS	SCHOOL/ WORK

MY TOP THREE POSITIVE COPING STRATEGIES.	STRESSORS OR PROBLEMS I HAVE RIGHT NOW.	HOW COULD I IMPROVE THE PROBLEM OR DECREASE THE STRESS?
1.		
2.		
3.		

MY *EMERGENCY* CARE SELF-CARE PLAN

LIST YOUR TOP FIVE EMERGENCY SELF-CARE PRACTICES.	MAKE A LIST OF THE RESOURCES AVAILABLE TO YOU AND PEOPLE AT SCHOOL/IN THE COMMUNITY TO WHOM YOU CAN TURN FOR HELP.
1.	
2.	
3.	
4.	
5.	

want to try. Have them list what they could do to cope when they start to feel overwhelmed.

Remind students that they can use their self-care plan even when they are not in your class. They can revise and use it at their discretion as new barriers appear, new coping tools are learned, and new life circumstances arise. That way the next time an earth-shaking moment hits them, they'll have a plan, and it might be just enough to keep their world from crumbling.

ASSET-BASED EDUCATION

An asset-based approach helps build students up and offers them healing by focusing on their strengths, not on what they lack. This approach is vital in fostering healing. Why? Our relationships show us how we should see the world, and they show us how we should view ourselves in the context of others. Trauma can be isolating, and depending on the type of trauma, it can lower a person's self-worth.[10] In order to create strong attachments, people who experience trauma need to feel secure and have a sense of self-worth. Sadly, education typically takes a deficit-based approach, highlighting students' weaknesses. Students get grouped by what they are *not* good at. Low in math. A behavior problem. No social skills. This context does not value a student nor build up self-worth. In this context, a student will learn to view themselves by what they lack. There is nothing in that situation for a child to cling to and learn from. I honor that we do need to help children with areas of weakness, but they need a strength-based environment in which to grow.

> Our relationships show us how we should see the world, and they show us how we should view ourselves in the context of others.

A former student taught me a Zulu greeting that truly symbolizes the daily goal of asset-based teaching with students: "*Sawubona.*" The greeting means "I see you, you are important to me, and I value you." It's based on the idea of constantly looking at a person with fresh eyes and without grudges, prejudice, and bias. The greeting serves as a reminder that every time we see a person, we should interact with them with appreciation and understanding. Some days student behaviors and actions may cloud our thoughts with negativity. That's why it's important to hold on to the idea of *sawubona* and seek to see past individual moments to discover the worth a person brings with them. It's a reminder that every life brings value to the world.

For example, if a flower lacks blooms and is wilting, we don't attempt to fix the flower. We don't focus on the lack of blooms. The first reaction is to try to fix the environment the flower grows in. Water the flower. Move it to better light. We try to help the flower gain strength. We need to do the same for students. We can't "fix" a person, but we can give them a foundation to thrive. With an asset-based approach, diversity in thought, culture, and traits are seen as positive assets. A person is valued for what they bring to school rather than being designated by what they lack or need to work on. An asset-based approach seeks to unlock student potential by focusing on talents.

An asset-based approach seeks to unlock student potential by focusing on talents.

UNDERSTANDING AND PERSONAL CONNECTIONS

It has to be said that understanding takes time and patience. We should not seek to force students to give us information. That devalues them. Understanding means a person tells their story, but only when they're ready. If a child has experienced trauma and we are aware of it, we should not focus on it. We don't want to cause a student to re-experience the trauma. We need to allow students to open up when they're ready. And while we wait, we need to provide a classroom environment that helps kids see the assets they bring with them.

One way to gain understanding, show students the assets they contain, and build relationships is through personal connections. We need to create learning tasks that validate students by incorporating their experiences, interests, passions, ethnicity, and culture. Give each student voice, choice, and an opportunity for personal connection.

We need to create learning tasks that validate students by incorporating their experiences, interests, passions, ethnicity, and culture.

To incorporate personal connections in the classroom, a teacher needs to look at the skill or objective and then think, "How can I bring in student experiences, beliefs, cultures, or personal identities into this lesson?" For example, a math educator who is teaching fractions might have students bring in a recipe of their favorite home-cooked food. Students could share why they chose their recipe, bits about the dish, the cultural connection for them, or the recipe's personal meaning. After, they could manipulate the recipe to feed ten people. They would be adding fractions in the recipe to equal a new serving size. You could even create a class cookbook that each student could take home. Adding personal connections helps build class community and connections by highlighting the beautiful diversity in the classroom.

Using this lens also allows students to form connections. As students share tidbits of information, it builds comradery and community through the sharing of personal identity. It helps students who carry trauma focus on their value.

USING ASSETS FOR MOMENTS OF STRUGGLE

Let's say a student takes something from another student. A teacher might respond, "We don't take things. That's bad." The problem with this response is that it shames the student. What if the student had to steal food to survive? We don't want to shame students and push them away from connecting with us and the classroom community. Instead, we can take a more asset-based approach. In that same situation, the teacher could state an objective observation: "I see you took something from another student. Why?" Notice there is no judgment. The teacher stays objective and allows the student to explain their rationale. At the same time, it gives the teacher a chance to reinforce expectations set forth in the class community. We as teachers need to find ways to respond to behaviors that honor the student's background and allow the student a chance to help us understand them and see where they are coming from.

> We as teachers need to find ways to respond to behaviors that honor the student's background and allow the student a chance to help us understand them and see where they are coming from.

It also helps us gain tools to support students after discipline. In the above situation, the teacher might remind students to borrow supplies if needed, which will alleviate fear in the child who feels they don't have enough. A person with trauma who is learning new skills and forming new neural pathways is going to mess up and make mistakes. They are also going to need more support after a setback.

RESTORATIVE ASSET-BASED REINTEGRATION

Jordan was sensitive about her father possibly going to prison. A fellow student found out about her worries and chose to make fun of her. Without thinking, Jordan hit the other student and ended up out of school for a few days. This wasn't a matter of right or wrong, it was a matter of helping her keep her self-worth, assets, and values after a corrective moment. It's important to remind the student of their value to the classroom community upon their return. That way they associate the moment of discipline as a lapse in judgment and don't internalize shame and guilt.

There are two tools I use for positive asset-based reintegration to the classroom and classroom community support. Before Jordan returned to my class, I made it a point to list some of the positive assets she brought to the classroom. It's important to utilize this list to reinforce to the student their assets before they return to the classroom. You can call the student's home before they return, e-mail them, or give them a letter as they enter the door of the classroom. I usually start with "I value you in the classroom community for your ..." and list five or six attributes that are as specific or as broad as you want, such as artistic nature, kindness to others, humor, sharing of their colored pencils, or love of enchiladas. This small gesture is a positive primer to help the student successfully return and integrate back into the community after a mishap.

In another activity, I have students write their name on the top of a sheet of paper and leave it on their desks. Students switch desks and write one reason they value the student and sign their name. I let students read their lists when finished and then I collect them. I use a student's sheet upon reintegration or before a stressful moment such as a test to serve as a reminder to the student of their value to the class community. This enhances the student's sense of belonging and provides a reminder to the student that the class community doesn't see them for their mistakes or how they perform, but for who they are.

Asset-based education is a long-term fix that takes time, patience, and understanding. It creates a school culture of mutual respect and belonging. The asset-based approach seeks to build students up. It shows we believe in students, and that's important. If we believe in students, they'll learn to believe in themselves.

> Asset-based education is a long-term fix that takes time, patience, and understanding.

SAFETY AND HEALING

Creating a healing environment that promotes safety is imperative for schools. When a child feels safe it is a protective factor for them. It makes a shield for every student to carry against the stressful situations of the world.[11] It raises resilience. It's a game-changer—for all kids.

Creating protective factors such as safety changes the weighted impact of trauma. That's one of the reasons this book starts with forming schools and classrooms that promote healing. Utilizing multiple protective factors equips our students with resources—resources they can use to heal from trauma and safeguard themselves. That's why it's important to create schools that focus on practices and daily methods that foster healing.

> Utilizing multiple protective factors equips our students with resources—resources they can use to heal from trauma and safeguard themselves.

HEART TO HEART

QUESTIONS AND IDEAS FOR ACTION

Reflect, discuss with a group, or share your thoughts and create a dialogue on social media using the book's hashtag, #HOPEforEdu.

Questions

1. The list of warning signs of trauma is an important guide for identifying possible trauma. Who may need to know these warning signs? Why would it be important for them to know? How would providing a list of warning signs help teachers in a classroom?

2. Safety is the first step in helping those with trauma. What do you currently do in your own classroom, school, or organization to make people feel safe? What's something you could do better or more of to increase mental safety?

Ideas for Action

- Write a self-care plan and stick to it. If we want our students to follow one, we have to model what it looks like. Make sure to schedule time for yourself, your family, and the activities you love in your day-to-day life. If you put it on your calendar, you will make time for simple activities that can revitalize you and keep your mind at its best to help those in your care.

HEALING AND RESILIENCE

When someone experiences trauma, their sympathetic nervous system (SNS) goes on high alert, looking for threats. When you perceive a threat, your body responds to either neutralize or move away from this perceived threat. If we are truly in danger of losing our lives, this reflex is useful. However, most daily interactions are not dangerous but may be perceived as such by an overactive SNS. No matter the danger, when a person's mind perceives a threat (dire or not), their SNS activates and prepares to do battle or run from situations, people, or the safety of a classroom. Overactivity of the SNS is the cause of a lot of stress, anxiety, and reactivity.[12] Soothing the SNS with coping tools is the solution, which makes me think of Zoe.

Zoe was a student who had been through a lot in a few months' time. Her mother lost custody of her due to neglect, and she moved to live with her grandmother, leaving her friends and former life behind. Dad came in and out of the picture at will and separated her from her baby brother. Within minutes of walking into class on the first day, Zoe was sitting with her arms crossed over her chest. I welcomed students and began a small get-to-know you activity, asking basic questions about interests, family, and life. After reading the start of the sheet, Zoe got up, shoved her desk aside, and left the room. I stood stunned with twenty-five young faces staring at me. Immediately I called a fellow teacher to cover my room while I went and found Zoe.

She was huddled on the floor of the girl's bathroom, sobbing. I knew she was in the waves of feeling her SNS overwhelm her. Before I adopted my children, I might have pitied her and just wanted to get her back to class. People with trauma don't need pity or rescuing. As a teacher, you don't need to walk a mile in your student's shoes, but you do need to help them realize that in those shoes they can walk further and do more, and that they have more power than they ever realized. They need tools to cope while healing.

Plus, if I were to step in and regulate Zoe's mood, she would come to rely on me to be a source of regulation. I didn't want to teach her learned helplessness. I wanted to model tools she could take with her. A person who becomes skilled in making the transition from distress to calm has developed internal control and is no longer a victim to circumstances. So instead of pitying her I began to teach her tools to fill in the GAP: grounding, analyzing, and progress building.

> A person who becomes skilled in making the transition from distress to calm has developed internal control and is no longer a victim to circumstances.

Grounding

Grounding is a practice that can help a person in distress pull away from flashbacks, negative self-talk, bad memories, and difficult emotions. Grounding allows the brain to refocus on the present moment and provides an opportunity to shift from the fight–flight–freeze SNS to the relaxed learning brain or parasympathetic nervous system (PNS). Grounding can help those with trauma, anxiety, or PTSD.[13] It's a great tool for giving a person a sense of control over their reactions. Teaching a couple of grounding techniques to your class benefits all kids. A lot of the grounding techniques I show students end up in their emergency self-care plans.

Grounding is a practice that can help a person in distress pull away from flashbacks, negative self-talk, bad memories, and difficult emotions.

As Zoe sat sobbing on the bathroom floor, I decided to use the 5-4-3-2-1 grounding method with her. This method has a person use their five senses to ground themselves in the present moment and is easy to teach and use. Simply, it's identifying five things that can be seen, four things that can be felt, three things that can be heard, two things that can be smelled, and one thing that can be tasted.

"Zoe, look at the floor, it's such a pretty blue. Can you tell me four other things you see from down there?"

Her sobs slowed and she began to look around. "Well, umm . . . the bottoms of white toilets?"

"Great, Zoe! Keep going."

The sobs stopped and she began to peer around the room intently. "There are also silver pipes, black paper towel holders, and rectangular, shiny, reflective mirrors."

"Wonderful descriptions, Zoe. Now can you tell me four things you are touching or feeling?"

She sat up and looked to the floor. "I feel the smooth floor and its bumps. I also feel fuzzy socks on my feet. Oh, and I feel the bracelet and watch dangling on my arm."

"Zoe, what about three things you hear?"

She slowed her breath further and looked around to listen. "I hear the drip of the faucet, the hum of the lights, and my voice echoing. You know what's weird? I don't feel like I did when I came in here. Can we go back to class? I just didn't want to do that sheet because I don't see eye-to-eye with my family right now."

I nodded. As we walked, I explained grounding exercises and their purpose and told her that grounding is a way to relax so a person can self-regulate in order to think. I went over the full 5-4-3-2-1 technique and told her to use it any time she felt big emotions. Now Zoe had a new tool in her mental toolbox to cope.

There are two main types of grounding techniques: mental and physical. It's best to showcase both to students early in the year and take one or two minutes a month to remind students of a couple of the techniques. Encourage them to use whatever techniques they are comfortable with and that fit the situation they are in. Generally, if a student is doing a physical activity, a cognitive technique is best, and if a student is doing a cognitive activity, a physical technique is best. For example, I tell my students that if they are about to take a big test, they might consider doing the physical breathing exercises so they don't get distracted while trying to think. Likewise, if they are about to run a big race it might be best to do a cognitive activity that will not disrupt a physical warm-up or exercise they are doing to prepare. Schools can showcase these techniques through morning announcements and posters to remind students that grounding is a tool to help them during moments of struggle. Figure 2.4 presents a list of other mental and physical grounding techniques that can be taught to and used by students.

FIGURE 2.4   GROUNDING TECHNIQUES

PHYSICAL
AND
MENTAL

GROUNDING TECHNIQUES TO HELP A PERSON SOOTHE AND COPE

ADAPTED FROM GROUNDING TECHNIQUES AT: HTTPS://WWW.THERAPISTAID.COM/WORKSHEETS/GROUNDING-TECHNIQUES.PDF

PHYSICAL

Take five long, deep breaths through your nose and exhale through your lips.

Clench your hands into fists, then release the tension. Repeat this ten times.

Reach your hands over your head like you're trying to reach the sky. Stretch like this for five seconds. Bring your arms down and let them relax at your sides.

Place both feet flat on the floor. Wiggle your toes. Curl and uncurl your toes several times. Spend a moment noticing the sensations in your feet.

MENTAL

Describe the steps in performing an activity you know how to do well.

Read something backwards, letter by letter. Practice for at least a few minutes.

Pick up an object and describe it in detail. Describe its color, texture, size, weight, scent, and any other qualities you notice Also, list all the ways the object can be used.

Think of an object and "draw" it in your mind, or in the air with your finger. Try drawing your home, a vehicle, or an animal.

SOURCE: Adapted from Therapist Aid. (2018). *Grounding techniques*. https://www.therapistaid.com/worksheets/grounding-techniques.pdf

ANALYZING AND PROGRESS BUILDING

Grounding is a great way to start helping students gain autonomy over their mental well-being. Once a person has strategies to cope with emotional triggers, it's important to figure out what prompts reactions in the first place. Analyzing allows a student to step back and observe their own behaviors reflectively and to figure out what triggers them, what their patterns of behavior are, and how to employ preventative measures detached from the moment of emotion.

Analyzing allows a student to step back and observe their own behaviors reflectively and to figure out what triggers them, what their patterns of behavior are, and how to employ preventative measures detached from the moment of emotion.

Analyzing should be done over the course of a few days to a week. It can be done through journaling (on paper or through video), by checking in with a student for a few minutes at the end of a school day, or by giving a student a sheet to track their reactions. No matter the method you choose, it's your job to help the student look objectively at their day to find patterns and triggers.

Zoe needed to know when to apply her newfound grounding tools. She understood from the bathroom incident that she could use grounding when she felt like she was going to "blow up." It's important to teach that any overwhelming feeling is a chance to use coping tools. Every student should have the power to use analyzing behaviors to increase their well-being. Over the course of the third or fourth week of school, I have all my students use the sheet presented in Figure 2.5.

Students reflect at the end of a day on the things that caused big emotions for them. First, they go back and recall where and about when the big emotion occurred. They try to pinpoint what caused the emotion to happen. Then they explain how they responded to the emotion. What did they do because of feeling that emotion? Next, they look to see if any patterns existed in their behaviors that day or over the course of several days. What did the behaviors have in common? Did a certain action or event cause them? Lastly, if they notice any patterns, trends, or repeated behaviors, they list possible preventative measures.

I gave Zoe this sheet to complete a week before I introduced analyzing to all my students. She noticed that whenever her friends or teachers started asking about family it made her feel angry and tense. She didn't react, but it still caused distress. The preventative measure she came up with was "politely ask my teachers and friends to not ask me about my family life and explain to them it will upset me." She implemented the plan. Later, she told me that she felt better than ever because people were not constantly bringing up family questions. Zoe also

FIGURE 2.5 TRIGGER, RESPONSE, PATTERNS, AND PREVENTION

ANALYZING MY WEEK

Fill out this analysis daily for a week. If you have no big emotions or triggers, leave it blank.

WHEN AND WHERE	TRIGGER	RESPONSE	PATTERNS	PREVENTION
Write when, were, and the time a big emotion occurred.	List any event that triggers a big emotion or behavioral response.	How did you respond? Did you exhibit a specific behavior?	Do you notice any patterns, trends, or habits? What are they?	Is there anything you could do in the future to prevent a negative trigger from happening?
Monday				
Tuesday				
Wednesday				
Thursday				
Friday				

realized while doing this that waiting until the day before a test to study caused her extreme anxiety. Her preventative measure? To study her notes every night to avoid anxiety. Analyzing allowed her to see the behaviors and triggers without emotion.

Students should be encouraged to come up with academic goals before major assignments and personal goals that will help them get there. More specific resources on goals and goal setting are found in the next chapter, but a key part of goal setting is making sure students track their progress. By having them set and use goals for their problems you are introducing a foundational component to hope. This small practice puts the student in control and helps them realize they have the power to shape who they become.

> Students should be encouraged to come up with academic goals before major assignments and personal goals that will help them get there.

As students come up with goals it's important to use progress building as they reach for those goals. It's the last but one of the most important parts to help students cope and heal. Changing behaviors and habits and strengthening new neural pathways takes time. Healing is not an endpoint, but a journey. We all want instant results, but the reality is real work takes time. That's why it's important students constantly look at how far they've progressed to gain intrinsic motivation to keep going. As Zoe set goals, I gave her a progress sheet to keep track of her progress. Progress charting helps students see how small changes can have a big impact on their well-being and positively reinforces the small wins in a big habit or behavior change. It allows the student to see they have control of their life and can change it.

> Progress charting helps students see how small changes can have a big impact on their well-being and positively reinforces the small wins in a big habit or behavior change.

Progress tracking can be done with the help of a teacher, by a student on their own digitally, or on a copied sheet of paper. I use the progress chart in Figure 2.6. Students use one sheet to state their goal, make plans to implement that goal, and track milestones. They also have a "help" section for problem solving. If a student gets stuck, I suggest they seek help from me or a fellow peer. They keep the sheet and track their goal until they have reached whatever measurable target they set for themselves. I ask my students to let me know their progress so I can celebrate their "small wins" with them. These little celebrations open the door to building positive connections with students.

FIGURE 2.6   GOAL PROGRESS

BEHAVIOR AND HABIT GOAL PROGRESS

Goal: State your goal.

Getting there: How will you get there? What are measurable and attainable mini-goals?

Tasks:	Target Dates:

Milestones: List any big moment of success and how it made you feel.

Milestones:	Feeling and reaction to milestones:

Plan if I need help or I get stuck:

QUESTIONS AND IDEAS FOR ACTION

Reflect, discuss with a group, or share your thoughts and create a dialogue on social media using the book's hashtag, #HOPEforEdu.

Questions

1. Coping doesn't erase pain, but it helps the person get through a moment. It's important to have students share their coping tools so staff can support them. Coping strategies may take a few minutes, so it's important staff recongizes this and allows the student the necessary time to regulate. What are the ways your school or grade level supports students trying to cope?

2. Behavior and habit change can be difficult. It's important to celebrate students through progress building. How can your school, classroom, or grade-level team celebrate or encourage students as they work to improve their personal well-being?

Ideas for Action

- When someone is identified as experiencing trauma, they need a lot of extra support. What systems, programs, and people can you utilize to provide support for those experiencing trauma? Create a plan of action and support that you can use to provide extra communication, consistency, and control to individuals in need.

 **HEART TO HEART**

QUESTIONS AND IDEAS FOR ACTION

Reflect, discuss with a group, or share your thoughts and create a dialogue on social media using the book's hashtag, #HOPEforEdu.

Questions

1. Peer connections are vital to supporting healing. Strong classroom communities help heal and foster student connections. What can you do to support community building outside of providing classroom lessons that are asset based?

2. As students heal from trauma, they may act out with you more because they feel secure in their relationship with you. What classroom or school community principles can you use to set guidelines and parameters for students with trauma?

Ideas for Action

- Asset-based education starts with looking at the language we use with students. People naturally have a built-in negativity bias. That sometimes comes across in the language, documents, and activities we use with students. For a single class period or over the course of a day, chart the amount of negative versus positive language you use. Then make a goal to increase the positive. The more intentional we are, the more supportive our classroom environment becomes.

Compassion for Colleagues

Healing: Supporting School Staff

It's easy to get overwhelmed by students' struggles. According to the 2016 National Survey of Children's Health, "34 million children ages 0–17—nearly half of all US children—had at least one of nine ACEs, and more than 20 percent had two or more."[1] Add on top of that other forms of trauma people may experience, such as natural disasters, bullying, and medical trauma. This reveals two certainties: We will deal with a lot of kids who carry trauma, and a vast majority of staff members have probably experienced trauma too. In addition, working day in and day out with students in pain takes a toll. After struggling with worry for your students, dealing with daily reminders of the problems facing them, and feeling an overwhelming desire to support and relieve them all, some educators begin to suffer symptoms of compassion fatigue. If left unchecked this condition can rob classrooms and schools of amazing educators. My goal in this section is to help you find ways to implement concepts from each chapter to help yourself and your colleagues avoid burnout and a feeling of just surviving. We want to help our students with mental wellness, and to do that we have to model school cultures of mental wellness.

> We want to help our students with mental wellness, and to do that we have to model school cultures of mental wellness.

The first step in promoting a culture of mental wellness is knowing how to recognize when you or a colleague may need help. With adults, symptoms of trauma or compassion fatigue may look different, and we may not even know we need help. For example, when I started caring for my new children, I went to school in a dazed state. It was hard to deal with my kids' stories of abuse and neglect and then go to school and help more students with pain and trauma. I stuck to lesson plans like a map and checked out mentally from the classroom. I listed objectives, followed procedures, graded papers, and slowly stopped caring. Overwhelmed, I sunk into my classroom walls of isolation and exhaustion. My health deteriorated and I blamed it on not being a good enough teacher. During one of my kid's therapy appointments, the mental health provider pointed out that I did not look well. On the spot, I told the therapist the entire story of how I had been feeling: I felt drained, I wanted to sleep to numb the sense of being overwhelmed, and I felt empty and thought I wasn't cut out for teaching. That's when I discovered compassion fatigue. Whereas students might overtly act out, staff members experiencing trauma or compassion fatigue more often than not experience symptoms associated with physical and emotional exhaustion.[2] Below is a list of various signs of adult trauma and compassion fatigue.

> Whereas students might overtly act out, staff members experiencing trauma or compassion fatigue more often than not experience symptoms associated with physical and emotional exhaustion.

Signs of Adult Trauma and Compassion Fatigue

- Anxiety, fear, and worry about their and others' safety
- Worry about recurrence or consequences of violence
- Changes in behavior
- Withdrawal from others or activities
- Absenteeism
- Increase in impulsivity, risk-taking behavior
- Discomfort with feelings (such as troubling thoughts of revenge)
- Increased irritability or impatience with students
- Difficulty planning classroom activities and lessons
- Decreased concentration
- Denying that traumatic events impact students or feeling numb or detached
- Intense feelings and intrusive thoughts that doesn't lessen over time about a student's trauma

According to the American Institute of Stress, "Compassion fatigue also called 'vicarious traumatization' or secondary traumatization is the emotional residue or strain of exposure to working with those suffering from the consequences of traumatic events."[3] Most of us went into education because of a deep compassion for humanity. You care deeply, and when others hurt, you step up to give. Compassion makes us feel a need to sacrifice, but there comes a point in which we can overwhelm our emotional and physical health. Caring too much can hurt.

> Compassion makes us feel a need to sacrifice, but there comes a point in which we can overwhelm our emotional and physical health.

We can't pour from empty cups, but often teachers and administrators feel the need to give until they can't. Mustafa Ataturk once said, "A good teacher is like a candle—it consumes itself to light the way for others." This quote is a perfect example of how compassion makes us feel the need to self-sacrifice until we are no more. However, for those of you thinking this is a noble pursuit, let me put it this way: You help more people when you're at your best. A full tank of gas goes farther than an empty tank. Staff members with trauma and compassion fatigue can't work as effectively, and that means that the school will not work as productively. A brain in pain works overtime and therefore cannot handle the same cognitive load. We don't have to give up our own mental health to light a path for others. It's similar to how on an airplane you are instructed to put on your own oxygen mask before helping others. Help yourself to safety and well-being first so you can help others.

> Help yourself to safety and well-being first so you can help others.

As we help our students, we need to be able to help ourselves and provide support for our colleagues. By taking the time to focus on the mental well-being of staff, we can perpetuate cultures of self-care and mental wellness. If we expect students to take care of their own well-being, we as adults must model it in our schools.

Communication, Consistency, and Control: Support

Educators spend much of their time distanced from colleagues. We work in classrooms and offices in which we are often the only adult in a given space. We might get together for meetings and curriculum work, but we need to purposely connect and form support networks for our mental well-being. It's important that you find a professional community of trusted colleagues with whom you can share your stress, hopes, encouragement, and victories.

> It's important that you find a professional community of trusted colleagues with whom you can share your stress, hopes, encouragement, and victories.

In fact, our brains are hardwired with a need to form communities of social support.[4] Much like educators form professional learning communities (PLCs) to improve their practice it's just as vital that we create professional support communities (PSCs) for mental well-being. This can be done individually or in a whole school setting.

To start forming a PSC you need to look for allies to assist you through difficult times: administrators, school secretaries, custodians, or the teacher next door. Take stock in the supportive relationships that you have in the building. If you have a mentor, grade-level team, or department that acts as a strong support, feel free to list them. Such relationships not only support you but can provide you with pathways and encouragement when you feel overwhelmed.

You can also build systems of communication to help expand personal support into the school network. For example, as a staff, you might implement a simple e-mail system to signify the need for a colleague's help, or staff members might use the door hanger outside of their door if they need someone to check in with them. Colleagues should be encouraged to send an e-mail or use some other method to seek out purposeful interaction with colleagues indicating they want a check-in. Noticing the door hanger or reading the e-mail should prompt others to seek out the staff member who may need a little encouragement or someone to listen.

Principals should walk the building a couple of times a day and provide aid to staff who may need a bit of extra help. Some staff members might be hesitant to use the door hangers, so think about simultaneously starting an e-mail signaling system with the words *mental check-in* as the subject line. Staff could list the reason they need support in the body of the e-mail or leave it blank if overwhelmed. This could help signal staff, administration, and school counselors to check in.

Also, like the students, consider creating your own self-care plan. List activities that make you feel better, your support networks, and the resources that are at your disposal to help in a time of need. Sharing your self-care plan with trusted colleagues ensures that they can assist you further in a time of crisis. Everyone is going to have bad days, but by creating systems of support and self-care, we can get through them together.

> Sharing your self-care plan with trusted colleagues ensures that they can assist you further in a time of crisis.

CHAPTER 3

OVERCOMING

"I just can't do it." Hannah lowered her head on her desk, signaling defeat. I looked down at her paper. The directions asked her to recall and write about a favorite childhood memory. The paper was blank.

I knelt next to her desk and whispered, "What can't you do? How can I help?"

She covered her head with her arms and mumbled, "All of it. I just can't do it. All the other kids are working. I just don't get writing. I'll never get it. I'm stupid at writing."

Maybe you have experienced being Hannah, or perhaps you've run into someone else who has just stopped trying. The world has become limited and possibilities have dried up. I felt hopelessness strongly a year after my husband and I adopted our children. At the end of the school year, I opted to take professional development training on adverse childhood experiences (ACEs) to help both my students and my own children. The first slide the speaker clicked on was full of statistics on ACEs and their correlations with predicted life outcomes. The slide contained two pictures, one of a prison cell and one of a graduation ceremony. The statistics hit home and made me feel helpless. The research showed that having experienced four or more ACEs was more strongly correlated with going to prison than graduating high school.

My children popped into my head. Their past had the potential to steal their future. I listened intently for answers on how to combat the effects of ACEs. The presentation gave only two solutions: trauma prevention and forming healthy relationships. Cultivating great relationships is a powerful tool. If a teacher forms great relationships with students, it can be a vital step toward helping those with trauma.

If a teacher forms great relationships with students, it can be a vital step toward helping those with trauma.

Preventing ACEs is equally as powerful, but for my kids, the damage had already been done. I had a good relationship with my kids. Would that be enough? Was there something else that could be done to fight ACEs and ensure that someone affected by them wouldn't end up as another statistic?

ATTRIBUTIONS AND LEARNED HELPLESSNESS

The answer came while reading research experiments conducted by Dr. Martin Seligman and Dr. Steven Maier in the 1960s. In the research studies, Seligman and Maier worked to classically condition dogs to the sound of a bell. When the bell would ring, the researchers administered a noninjurious electric shock to two experimental groups of dogs. One dog set was provided with a button that, when pushed, would turn the shock off. The other dogs had no button. After the dogs were conditioned, the researchers placed both groups in a new environment.

The dogs were put in a box divided into two spaces by a small partition. One side of the box had an electric floor and the other side did not. The dogs were put on the side of the box with the electric floor. When the bell rang, they received a shock from the floor. In this new environment, the dogs could easily jump over the small partition to get to the safe side of the box. The researchers expected both sets of dogs to hear the bell and jump over the partition after being shocked, escaping the electric floor. They believed self-preservation would kick in despite previous conditioning, but that didn't happen.

The dogs who'd had the button in the previous experiment quickly looked around and jumped to safety. However, the dogs who hadn't had the button didn't even try to move. When they felt the shock, they stopped moving, put their heads down on the floor, and whimpered helplessly. They just sat there, letting the shocks happen. The researchers realized the dogs had learned that helplessness from the first part of the experiment. Their past experience had taught them that they could not avoid the shock, so when they felt the shock in a new environment, they gave up. The past experience determined the dogs' future.

Further research[1,2] has shown that the way a person views adverse events that happen to them impacts whether they feel helpless or not. These views are what psychologists call attributions. A person's attributions are the factors they blame for the outcome of a situation. We make them every day for positive and adverse events. For example, imagine you just failed a test in history. There are several reasons you could list for failing: You could say you didn't study hard enough, you could claim the test was unfair, or, like Hannah, you could call yourself stupid. Each of those reasons is a different type of attribution.

Psychologists have discovered three specific attributions that cause learned helplessness[3]: internal, stable, and global. The first attribution was demonstrated by Hannah when she called herself stupid at writing. She was angry at herself for not knowing how to start the assignment in class and blamed her intelligence. These thoughts are internal attributions that happen when a person sees themselves as the cause of something happening. Hannah blamed her struggle with writing as the cause of all her problems.

Psychologists have discovered three specific attributions that cause learned helplessness: internal, stable, and global.

Stable attributions don't change across time or situations. Hannah's belief that she is stupid at writing and will always be stupid at writing is a stable attribution. This stable attribution will be uppermost in her mind before starting any writing assignment. She will start with the idea that she does not have the means to write because of her lack of skill. She will see her lack of skill as a permanent barrier to her ability to write. This will cause Hannah to give up on any writing assignment before even entering a classroom, similar to the dogs in the experiment.

If Hannah thought she was stupid in every aspect of life and not just her schooling, this attribution would be global. A global attribution is a belief that the factors affecting an outcome apply to many situations. Global attributions are held belief structures that a person utilizes in all daily interactions. This attribution would be with Hannah every second of the day and impact every exchange and decision in her life. It would cause her to back down from challenges as she would see herself as not equipped to face the trials of life. This would hinder Hannah from living up to her potential.

A global attribution is a belief that the factors affecting an outcome apply to many situations.

The biggest problem with negative internal, stable, and global attributions is they can become self-fulfilling prophecies. For example, Hannah thinks that she is stupid at writing, so when she gets a writing assignment, she doesn't even attempt to start. She stops trying to do well in writing and therefore gets a bad grade. For Hannah, this validates the fact that she is stupid at writing. What Hannah doesn't see is that because she gave up, she continues to struggle with writing. Her attributions have created a cycle of learned helplessness that appears to prove Hannah right. She doesn't set goals, she doesn't try to find a way around the problem, and she has no motivation to try. Helpless. Hopeless.

Any person can form attributions that hinder success. All of our students are susceptible, but ACEs and trauma can increase the chance of developing attributions that lead to helplessness. Trauma impacts the way a person thinks about themselves. My children's biological parents continually berated them, labeling them dumb and worthless. Their parents saw them as an inconvenience. They were expected to take care of each other, be quiet, and scavenge for food amongst piles of trash bags. When any of them stepped out of line, they faced an onslaught of physical and verbal abuse.

All of our students are susceptible, but ACEs and trauma can increase the chance of developing attributions that lead to helplessness.

This environment reinforced that they could not succeed. Over and over, they would try to change the world around them. They set goals to be quieter, less of a burden, and kinder, all to get love from their parents. Despite their best efforts, every day they would wake up to the same struggles. No matter what they tried, they couldn't change their parents. They couldn't get the love they wanted. This cycle built internal attributions that led to utter hopelessness. They believed there was no point in trying.

My kids went to school and struggled at first. They saw no point in trying because they believed everything was their fault. If they got a bad grade, they thought it was because they were not quite good enough, not lovable enough, not smart enough. Their previous environment taught them to believe they would never be enough. Even when the environment changed, the negative attributions remained. Like the dogs in the experiment, they entered the new environment and put their heads down when challenges arose. They accepted failure because their previous environment taught them it was inevitable.

Childhood trauma negatively influences an individual's internal representation of self[4] and the attributions they form. When they failed at something, my children believed it was just the world's validation that their birth parents were right and they were worthless. Their academic struggles became self-fulfilling prophecies. If they failed, they blamed themselves. If they succeeded, they saw it as a lucky break that had nothing to do with their capabilities. Their internal representations reinforced negative attributions, causing them to feel stuck and helpless.

Childhood trauma negatively influences an individual's internal representation of self and the attributions they form.

Initially, a person wanders into the forest of learned helplessness and adverse attributional styles because of a negative experience. Something caused them to move deep into the woods as their mind casually drifted into a new way of thinking. The person may have paused for a moment, and they became stuck when they looked to find their way back.

Hannah likely didn't always feel like she was bad at writing. She wandered in the woods too long. She kept circling on the same thought until she became lost and only knew that she wound up back in the same spot whenever she tried to escape. My children didn't give up trying right away. They tried and failed over and over. Over time their willpower depleted and they laid down on the forest floor and gave up trying. Something guided them into the woods. Now they were lost and stuck.

How would you feel? Scared? Certainly. Anxious? To put it mildly. Angry? I could understand that. It's frustrating getting stuck on a path that doesn't get you anywhere. But most of all, what about helpless? No idea where to go. No feeling of what to do. No one would blame you for wanting to stop, curl up into a ball on the forest floor, and just stop trying. You are overwhelmed with the thought that you will never get out of the woods. Freeze-frame that emotion for a moment.

Can you sense for just a second how it feels to be out of your element? Out of solutions? Out of exits? Can you imagine how it feels to be out of hope?

That's why telling a student just to try something can be terrifying to them. It's not success that terrifies them. What they're afraid of is trying to get out of being stuck and winding up back in that same spot. This would prove to them that there is no way out. It's essential to find the children who feel like this because, for many students, life is a forest. Not a forest of dark trees and pricker bushes. But briars and thickets full of broken hearts, failed attempts, and discouragement. Their predators are not animals but the thoughts that they are not good enough, not smart enough, simply just not enough. The uncertainty of getting lost deeper in hopelessness terrifies them.

That's why students need more than just encouragement to find a way out of helplessness. Telling a kid that "failure isn't the end, never give up, keep trying" and putting up posters on perseverance isn't enough. We can't relegate students' psychological and emotional health to one part of a school day in a social-emotional learning lesson. Changing attributions requires focus, support, and reinforcement to help new models and attributions stick.

Changing attributions requires focus, support, and reinforcement to help new models and attributions stick.

We can't improve a student's psychological state with a poster or generic encouragement. Children need support. They need a guide out of the woods. This is the reason having a measure that shows how deep a student is in the forest is critical. Then you can see what a student needs to re-energize their educational journey. It can give you specific tools, strategies, and interventions to support them. To guide them. To motivate them. To help them finally get up off the forest floor and find a way out.

HOPE: USING HOPE SCORES TO FOSTER RESILIENCE FROM SETBACKS, TRAUMA, AND ACEs

Up to now we've been following the stories of my children, Hannah, and the group of dogs who lost hope and faith in themselves after repeated failures. Despite being stuck in hopelessness, this is not where their stories end. Remember, there was another group of dogs. They received shocks too, but when they were moved to the new environment, they escaped. They didn't remain in the forest of helplessness. They had the answers needed to get out of the forest. What of this group?

This group of dogs had a different experience in the first part of the experiment. The small button that stopped the shocks gave them a pathway to getting out of the situation, and they developed agency/willpower to reach their goal of escape. They still received a shock, but that button helped them realize they had power. That adversity did not define them. Through hope and optimism they learned that in the end, they could change the world around them. They discovered that the more pathways they tried, the more likely they could find a way out. It gave them the motivation to keep pursuing their goals. Just a tiny bit of hope went a long way. The experiment showed that how we interpret our experiences colors the reality we perceive.

The dogs who learned optimism gained hope and fared better in the experiment. Similarly, people who have higher hope scores have better life outcomes. Higher hope is related to better outcomes in athletics, physical health, psychological adjustment, and life satisfaction.[5] A person's hope level has also been shown to be the most robust predictor of GPA, graduation rates, and academic achievement when controlling for educational history.[6] Instilling hope through learned optimism provides psychological capital that can be used to overcome future trials. It helps all people fare better, but could it be used to combat the effects of ACEs?

> Higher hope is related to better outcomes in athletics, physical health, psychological adjustment, and life satisfaction.

A research study by Hellman and Gwinn reveals strengthening hope can do more than combat ACEs. It can change lives. Hope acts as a psychological resource to mitigate trauma and works to improve outcomes and overall success. Strengthening hope leads to those with ACEs improving their skills, resiliency, and overall self-esteem.[7] Hope can help those with trauma and ACEs thrive.

> Strengthening hope leads to those with ACEs improving their skills, resiliency, and overall self-esteem.

In their study, Hellman and Gwinn analyzed the effects of teaching hope at a summer camp to children with ACEs who had been exposed to domestic violence. They measured children's hope using the Children's Hope Scale throughout the summer. They found that hope acted as a protective resource that helped the children cope with stress and adversity.

The higher the hope the child gains, the greater their capacity to identify viable pathways around problems to meet their goals. The researchers found that in this study, increased hope was related to striving for opportunities (zest, grit, optimism, curiosity), the ability to regulate thoughts and feelings (self-control), and understanding and appreciating the actions, motives, and feelings of others (social intelligence, gratitude). Further studies on the power of hope show that higher hope in students mediates the relationship between socioeconomic status and academic achievement.[8] Hope helps level the playing field of opportunity by offering a child their most incredible resource: their own resourcefulness. It's even been shown to assist in alleviating systematic inequalities in higher education.[9] Hope acts in the brain as a personal asset to help a person learn and grow despite the circumstances they face.

A 2017 neuroimaging study revealed that hope has a significant impact on higher brain functioning.[10] Hope affects a person's medial orbitofrontal cortex (mOFC). The mOFC is responsible for reward-related processing, motivation production, problem-solving, and goal-directed behaviors. In resting-state fMRI scans of adolescent brains, researchers found hope was connected to how the mOFC runs. A person's hope works in the brain to support the mOFC, which drives their will and ability to learn. So if the mOFC was the car of our thinking brain, hope is like a mechanic. The vehicle can still run with problems. However, having hope around as a mechanic ensures the mOFC runs smoothly. A brain can function without hope, but having hope helps when facing problems.

The researchers found this connection in their study when they discovered hope acted as a mediator between the mOFC and anxiety. So if the mOFC car runs into some anxiety potholes, hope, serving as a mechanic, starts work immediately to fix the car. Right on the spot. It doesn't mean anxiety won't happen, as we all face anxiety potholes. Sickness. Disasters. Death. Despite the potholes we encounter, hope is there to help a person back on the road to learning and mental wellness. Anxiety and trauma will happen. Hope regulates how much this will impact us and our thinking. Hope helps us get through tough times.

With hope acting as an asset for coping, psychological hope can only boost a person's chances of future success. For my children, measuring and strengthening hope would mean a chance to break free from being a statistic for ACEs. Hope won't help those with ACEs erase trauma to make a new beginning, but it can lessen the impact of trauma, giving them a shot to create a brand new ending.

Hope won't help those with ACEs erase trauma to make a new beginning, but it can lessen the impact of trauma, giving them a shot to create a brand new ending.

For Hannah and those with learned helplessness, hope would work to lower anxiety to allow them to learn new attributions. Stronger hope assists those with learned helplessness to get through adverse circumstances and learn not to be defined by them. Building hope through simple daily practices can change the world for those with trauma, anxiety, and learned helplessness. For students who are already hopeful, increasing hope further boosts their resilience and future success. Every person could use extra support, so every person's hope level matters.

Teaching hope and instilling learned optimism is not a program but simple practices that schools can adopt to increase mental wellness and success. Hope is easily measured and strengthened with intervention. We can improve well-being, resiliency, and achievement for all students by focusing on hope levels. Hope can be measured using the Children's Hope Scale or the Adult Hope Scale. The tests measure hope through a person's perceptions of their ability to reach their goals through two components: agency and pathways. Agency is the ability to work towards a goal (willpower), and pathways indicate the capacity to find a way towards the goal (waypower). The Children's Hope Scale is six items on a six-point Likert scale suitable for children ages eight to sixteen. The Adult Hope Scale is twelve items measured on a four-point Likert scale ideal for those seventeen and above. Both are free, take two to four minutes to complete, and require only the proper citations to use. They are reliable and valid and have been extensively tested in schools.[11]

> Agency is the ability to work towards a goal (willpower), and pathways indicate the capacity to find a way towards the goal (waypower).

FIGURE 3.1   THE CHILDREN'S HOPE SCALE

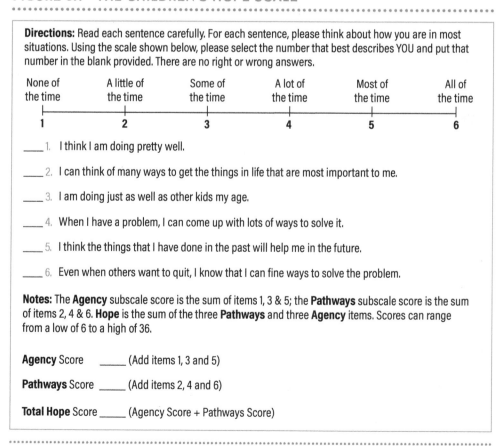

Directions: Read each sentence carefully. For each sentence, please think about how you are in most situations. Using the scale shown below, please select the number that best describes YOU and put that number in the blank provided. There are no right or wrong answers.

None of the time	A little of the time	Some of the time	A lot of the time	Most of the time	All of the time
1	2	3	4	5	6

_____ 1. I think I am doing pretty well.

_____ 2. I can think of many ways to get the things in life that are most important to me.

_____ 3. I am doing just as well as other kids my age.

_____ 4. When I have a problem, I can come up with lots of ways to solve it.

_____ 5. I think the things that I have done in the past will help me in the future.

_____ 6. Even when others want to quit, I know that I can fine ways to solve the problem.

Notes: The **Agency** subscale score is the sum of items 1, 3 & 5; the **Pathways** subscale score is the sum of items 2, 4 & 6. **Hope** is the sum of the three **Pathways** and three **Agency** items. Scores can range from a low of 6 to a high of 36.

Agency Score   _____ (Add items 1, 3 and 5)

Pathways Score _____ (Add items 2, 4 and 6)

Total Hope Score _____ (Agency Score + Pathways Score)

SOURCE: Snyder, C. R., Hoza, B., Pelham, W. E., Rapoff, M., Ware, L., Danovsky, M., Highberger, L., Ribinstein, H., & Stahl, K. J. (1997, June). The development and validation of the Children's Hope Scale, *Journal of Pediatric Psychology, 22*(3), 399–421. https://doi.org/10.1093/jpepsy/22.3.399

FIGURE 3.2 THE ADULT HOPE SCALE

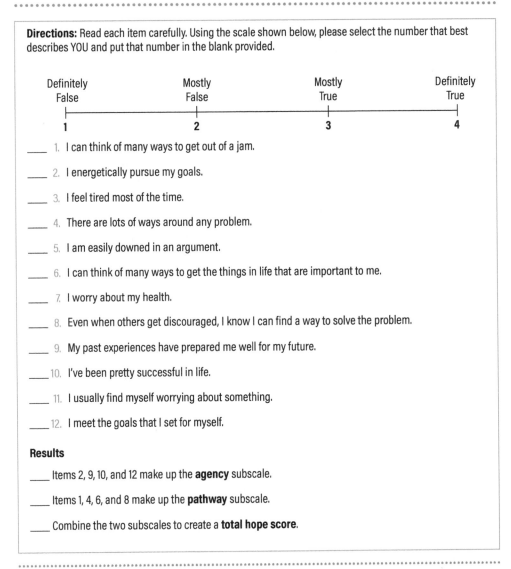

Directions: Read each item carefully. Using the scale shown below, please select the number that best describes YOU and put that number in the blank provided.

Definitely False	Mostly False	Mostly True	Definitely True
1	2	3	4

____ 1. I can think of many ways to get out of a jam.

____ 2. I energetically pursue my goals.

____ 3. I feel tired most of the time.

____ 4. There are lots of ways around any problem.

____ 5. I am easily downed in an argument.

____ 6. I can think of many ways to get the things in life that are important to me.

____ 7. I worry about my health.

____ 8. Even when others get discouraged, I know I can find a way to solve the problem.

____ 9. My past experiences have prepared me well for my future.

____ 10. I've been pretty successful in life.

____ 11. I usually find myself worrying about something.

____ 12. I meet the goals that I set for myself.

Results

____ Items 2, 9, 10, and 12 make up the **agency** subscale.

____ Items 1, 4, 6, and 8 make up the **pathway** subscale.

____ Combine the two subscales to create a **total hope score**.

SOURCE: Snyder, C. R., Harris, C., Anderson, J. R., Holleran, S. A., Irving, L. M., Sigmon, S. T., Yoshinobu, L., Gibb, J., Langelle, C., & Harney, P. (1991). The will and the ways: Development and validation of an individual-differences measure of hope. *Journal of Personality and Social Psychology, 60*(4), 570–585. https://doi.org/10.1037/0022-3514.60.4.570

At the start of the school year, I get all my students to fill out the Children's Hope Scale using a Google Form as a five-minute warm-up. Should a new student come during the year, I give them the test in a welcome packet along with a self-care plan to best support their resiliency and success. I like to read the items aloud and allow my students a few seconds to pick a rating representing them on the Likert scale. After they finish, I compile the results. The results come from tallying up the student's agency, pathways, and overall hope scores using the instructions on the test. The test is also easily adaptable to a Google Form, which allows results to be compiled quickly and efficiently. A Google Form would also help to monitor progress.

On the Children's Hope Scale, scores of thirty or above indicate that a child has high hope. Scores from eighteen to twenty-nine demonstrate hope at a moderate level. Scores from twelve to eighteen register hope but at moderate low levels. Scores below six put a student in a low-hope category that needs immediate intervention.

The test provides critical information to help differentiate and support hopefulness in students. When given intermittently throughout the year, The Children's Hope Scale can check progress for rising hope levels and spot possible problems. Erratic adverse fluctuations in hope can serve as an indicator of increasing distress levels. This test can help avoid letting those students with mounting issues fall through the cracks.

Think about your own journey. Was there a period of your life that was difficult that you dealt with on your own? Where you endured by just getting through the day-to-day? How would extra support have impacted you?

On top of helping identify struggling students, knowing a student's hope score can help educators plan students' support. Once you see a student's hope score, you can use the subscores and the overall score to help build hope in areas of weakness. After analyzing students' scores, educators can plan targeted interventions in their daily lessons to strengthen goals, agency, and pathways to foster hope. This can increase the ability of each student to learn content, gain more intrinsic motivation, and, most importantly, find more success and happiness at school.

> This can increase the ability of each student to learn content, gain more intrinsic motivation, and, most importantly, find more success and happiness at school.

The biggest takeaway from the experiment by Seligman and Maier is that hope matters. It plays an integral part in the attributions people form and whether they will give up or keep going. We know our students will face difficulties out in the world. By focusing on increasing hope, we are providing our students with a powerful psychological force that they can use out in the world against setbacks, adversity, and trials.

BUILDING HOPE: HOPEFUL MODELS

Providing guides and models that support psychological hope can help a child gain learned optimism. One of the most straightforward practices to increase hope levels for low-hope students is implementing student hope mentors. Psychological research has shown that students tend to have hope scores similar to those of people they associate with frequently. Promoting friendships and associations with peers who have higher hope has been shown to increase hope.[12]

Encouraging friendships with high-hope role models can help students learn new attributions, develop new problem-solving skills through collaboration, promote agency through partnered goals, and increase hope. Not everyone in your class will need a hope mentor. Students with moderate to high hope scores benefit more from thinking models and activities that promote goal setting, pathways, and agency. (These will be mentioned later in this chapter.) Students with lower hope gain hope quicker from having constant contact with other students who model hopeful thinking. Pairing a low-hope student with a hope mentor promotes friendship and gives the low-hope student access to a continuous model of how to use hope (goals, agency, and pathways) while learning.

When you decide to pair students, consider giving the low-hope student input on choosing a couple of higher-hope students they could collaborate with in the class. People don't always get along with each other, and if there is a high-hope person a child thinks they might work better with, give them a chance to choose their mentor. Because they had a choice, it may encourage them to use their mentor. Allowing students to sit next to or near their hope mentor gives them easy access to utilize their mentor. Encouraging students to engage with their hope mentor provides the student with scaffolding to gain higher-hope practices.

Encouraging students to engage with their hope mentor provides the student with scaffolding to gain higher-hope practices.

Having a hope mentor is the equivalent of having a knowledgeable guide show up in the forest of learned helplessness with a map and GPS. The guide could provide the lost person with advice and walk with them, providing support, reassurance, and feedback as they work to find a way out. The map would give the person struggling the confidence to take those first steps and reassurance that there is a way out. Higher-hope students can show off hopeful thinking and models for building hope, encouraging learned optimism and rising hope. Of course, students will be scared at first, but with mentors and strong models by their side, students will have support, guidance, and resources to leave the forest behind.

With mentors and strong models by their side, students will have support, guidance, and resources to leave the forest behind.

Hope Mentors and Models

I provide students a hopeful flowchart to help them get started and to guide mentors on what they should do in a hopeful partnership. Depending on the grade level or subject, you can modify the flowchart to suit your needs with pictures or simpler language. The point of the flowchart is to help students develop pathways and agency to get started. It also provides the low-hope students a guide of times they should utilize mentors.

FIGURE 3.3 HOPEFUL FLOWCHART

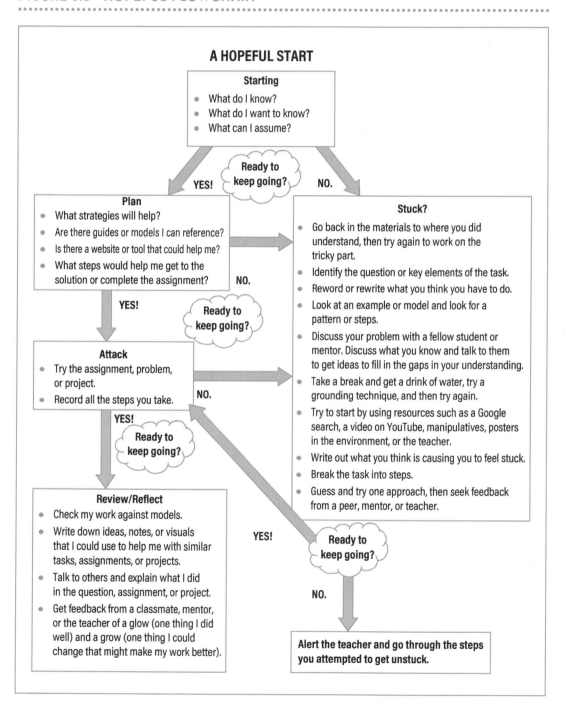

The flowchart assists students in employing learned optimism and works to strengthen pathways and agency. The first box gives students a place to start, which builds up agency and boosts confidence as it guides them. The flowchart questions and steps coach the student to break down what they are doing into goal-centered checkpoints. As students work through the flowchart, these checkpoints build success momentum as they conquer steps and problem-solve their way around stuck moments. Plus, it provides students with an immediate (attainable) action step that offers a high chance of success, thereby creating positive momentum as they continue to work through the problem.

You will also notice the flowchart promotes an environment of growth as students evaluate the resources available to them and find ways around problems. Lastly, using a flowchart with built-in mentors encourages students to work together and learn from each other's strengths and weaknesses as part of the learning process.

A hope mentor's role is to act as a resource for students during the lesson. That's why they appear as an option in the "Stuck?" column. Their job is to help students bypass roadblocks. When a student goes to another student seeking help, the pair uses hopeful collaboration to work together on an action plan for the problem. The mentor giving advice uses the listen-share-collaborate method to help problem-solve solutions. At the start of the school year, I go over hopeful collaboration with all students and do a modeled think-aloud with a student volunteer. Then I have students practice with a fake problem, such as feeling overwhelmed from losing an important item. The critical piece in this process is modeling—offering helpful collaboration versus giving someone a single answer. I like to tell students that this process is similar to coaching someone. If you give someone the direct answer, they can't learn, but if you help them find their way using guides and action steps, it builds their confidence, cements your learning and understanding, and helps you both build hope.

> If you help them find their way using guides and action steps, it builds their confidence, cements your learning and understanding, and helps you both build hope.

The first step in hopeful collaboration is to show students how to listen. Listening helps someone open up and build comfort and security with their partner. It also allows students to practice empathy and understand their partner's viewpoint. It's the equivalent of going into the woods of helplessness and sitting by the person's side. This small step provides security and reassurance. Also, talking about the problem with someone else allows a student time to process their stuck point. By asking clarifying questions and restating critical aspects of the conversation, the mentor helps the stuck person fully see the problem they are bringing to the table. I've seen many students go through the first step and then rush away from the collaboration because they just needed to discuss the problem in order to solve it.

> Listening helps someone open up and build comfort and security with their partner.

FIGURE 3.4   HOPEFUL COLLABORATION

1. Listen. *Learn about what the other person is thinking.*

Use questions to show you clearly understand the other person, restate the main points of their thoughts, and ask what they tried or what they are feeling.

2. Share. *Explain what you would do and your thinking process.*

After you have a complete understanding of what is going on with the other person, explain how you would approach the roadblock or obstacle. Also, point out additional resources the other person might use to help them get past their barrier.

3. Collaborate. *Work together to come up with an action plan to succeed.*

After you have come up with resources or possible pathways, develop an action plan to implement. Start with a plan that begins with: When I walk away from this conversation, I will _____ first. Next, I will _____. If I get stuck, I will _____.

Next, the mentors share pathways by explaining the ways they might tackle the problem. They also can use the "Stuck?" section of the flowchart to point out additional resources that a student could use to solve the issue. Each step gives a person new perspectives and pathways they can use to get past their stuck point.

Most importantly, after identifying a few pathways, the pair collaborates on an action plan for the stuck individual to use the moment they walk away. The action plan gives a student scaffolding to access high-hope goal setting, pathways, and agency to keep going.

Having levels of support built into the classroom environment encourages hope. It allows students to remain independent, gives them a chance to forge a path to mastery, and promotes confidence in their abilities. Plus, it shows students that being stuck isn't an endpoint in learning, just an opportunity to start a new journey.

The modeled process instills hope by utilizing mirror neurons. Having mentors go through a modeled process for hopeful collaboration and having the mentees reiterate the procedure allows the brains to get in sync. Hope mentoring allows the mirror neurons in the low-hope student to develop neural patterns similar to those of their mentors. Researchers have documented this mirroring process, which can be seen in this study on interbrain synchronization during social interaction.

Hope mentoring allows the mirror neurons in the low-hope student to develop neural patterns similar to those of their mentors.

FIGURE 3.5   BRAIN SYNCHING MIRROR NEURONS

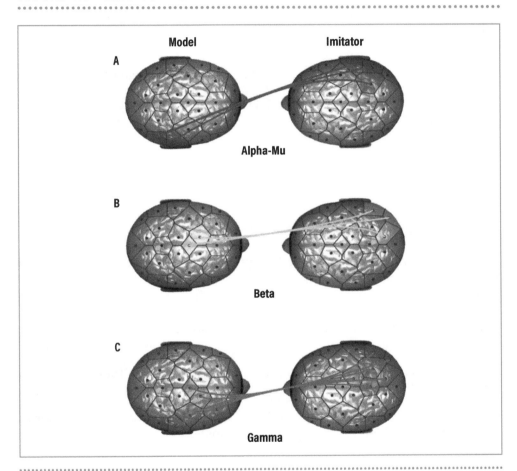

SOURCE: Dumas, G., Nadel, J., Soussignan, R., Martinerie, J., & Garnero, L. (2010, August 17). Inter-Brain Synchronization during Social Interaction. *PLoS ONE* 5(8), e12166. https://doi.org/10.1371/journal .pone.0012166

This process assists the low-hope student in coregulating their thoughts. The thoughts of the high-hope person become a pattern that builds over time in their own brain. Thought synchronization between a low-hope student and a high-hope model works to calm negative thought processes and produces a feedback loop that is soothing and hopeful for both students. The use of mirror neurons to help coregulate hope through modeling is visible in the brain and is immediately impactful.

Hannah was one in a large class of low-hope students. The hope mentors were only a point or two above each other at the start of the year. The vital thing to note is any higher-hope models can assist those with lower hope, including teachers. You can mentor students through their struggles just like hope mentors. When talking with Hannah, I used steps in hopeful collaboration to help her work through her problem.

> Any higher-hope models can assist those with lower hope, including teachers. You can mentor students through their struggles just like hope mentors.

"Hannah, I hear you say that you can't do the writing assignment. Why is that?"

Hannah looked down and whispered, "I just don't know where to start. I have too many childhood memories that I like. If I start writing about them, I will mess them up, and they will look dumb."

I nodded and repeated back the main points. "I hear you say you have a lot of childhood memories, but you are afraid that writing about them will hurt your memories."

She nodded and lifted her head. "Yeah."

"If I had to do this assignment, I would probably make a list of memories and write about the one that I could play back in my head like a movie. It would be hard to mess up the memory with lots of details that would make it seem real to others. Before writing, I might even talk about my memory to someone else to help me put the moment into words. You could also look under the 'Stuck?' list for other ideas of how to make your memory as accurate as you want it to be."

As Hannah considered these options, I asked, "What do you think would be a good first step?"

She sat back and rubbed her chin. "I think I may want to talk my top memories out and maybe take notes as I explain them, similar to what you suggested with the movie."

"That sounds like a great idea. You could even look at each memory and judge the number of details for the strength of the memory to help you choose your favorite."

She nodded. "Yes, and then I could use the details to write it!"

I smiled at her. "So, just to recap your action plan, you are going to talk about a few memories. As you talk about them, you are going to make a list of key points, and, once finished, you are going to look for the most detailed list and use that memory and that list for the assignment."

"Yep. I think I can do this."

Hannah talked about a few family vacations, taking notes on big ideas. Once she finished, she circled one and then looked up and said, "I think I got this now. You can go do teacher things. Oh, and umm, thanks."

Should students get stuck or feel helpless, hopeful collaboration with a mentor can help them gain momentum and promote learned optimism. It's not going to stop a person from occasionally feeling helpless, but it will remind them they have the power to change the situation. The guides and models can help students develop a grander vision, lifting their spirits in those moments of academic struggle, reassuring them that getting stuck isn't the end, giving them strength not to give up, and letting them know they can begin again.

Should students get stuck or feel helpless, hopeful collaboration with a mentor can help them gain momentum and promote learned optimism.

HEART TO HEART

QUESTIONS AND IDEAS FOR ACTION

Reflect, discuss with a group, or share your thoughts and create a dialogue on social media using the book's hashtag, #HOPEforEdu.

Questions

1. Hope mentors provide support and guidance to children with low hope. Reflect on your past and someone who mentored or guided you through a transition in your life. How did their support help you? Why do you think it's essential to have built-in social support as a child works to build hope?

2. What things in school could cause a child to get stuck in the woods of hopelessness? What could you do to prevent or combat this?

3. Why do you think hope is one of the most robust indicators of academic success? How has hope helped you through moments in your educational journey?

Ideas for Action

- Take the Adult Hope Scale and measure your hope score. Were the results surprising? In which area (agency or pathways) did you score highest? Do you feel your hope is an accurate reflection of your happiness and success?

- Create a flowchart for content areas, activities, or procedures in your school or classroom students could use. Use it to teach students to develop the pathways and agency you want them to possess to keep going.

GOALS: USING THE LEARNING GOAL CYCLE TO BUILD HOPE AND SUCCESS

Once students have a solid foundation to support hopefulness and learned optimism, the next step is increasing the components that make up hope: goals, agency, and pathways. On the hope scale, you will notice that goals don't receive a score. Why? Because people are naturally goal directed.

People set goals daily, from trying to win a game to mastering a new skill. Our goals can vary from concrete, such as riding a bike without training wheels, to vague, such as seeking fulfillment and happiness. The length of a person's goals can also vary from short term, such as finishing an assignment, to long term, such as losing weight. It's also possible to mix the two, with a person setting smaller subgoals to reach a larger goal.

Regardless of the type of goal, a key component of setting a goal is that the outcome should never be inevitable. If a person has a 100 percent chance or a 0 percent chance that a goal will turn out, goal setting for that activity is pointless. For example, you wouldn't say, "I hope to read the following sentence on this page," because you already know you have that ability. Certain things don't require hope. Goals that involve hope exist somewhere in the middle between an impossibility and a sure thing. The goals that build hope offer a challenge that causes growth.

Science has discovered a strong connection between goals and success. The research on goals confirms that we can achieve what we reach for, plan for, and believe in.[13] Goals declare to our minds and to others that we think we can reach a different future. The words and targets help us create a reality that doesn't exist. It's pretty miraculous if you think about it. Goals take a dream or desire and put it into words; a person creates a plan, and from that plan, the stuff of dreams takes shape. Goals breathe life into dreams. Goals help the impossible become a reality.

> The research on goals confirms that we can achieve what we reach for, plan for, and believe in.

Connection Between Goals and Future Success

Some of the greatest minds committed to their goals long before they were actually realized. For example, Martin Luther King Jr. committed to ending segregation and ensuring civil rights amid racial unrest in America. He sparked a movement that pushed President Lyndon Johnson to create laws ending segregation years after King first began pursuing his goal. You could also look at Thomas Edison, who told the world he would make a lightbulb almost a year before the first rays of light were birthed from the darkness. A person's hope level is critical in setting goals. The goals set by King and Edison exhibited high hope as the commitments they made were challenging and complex. A person's hope score impacts the type and number of goals they set for themselves and their belief in achieving those goals.

A person's hope score impacts the type and number of goals they set for themselves and their belief in achieving those goals.

Studies on hope, goals, agency, and pathways reveal that high-hope individuals take on more challenging goals. The reason why? A high-hope person uses their agency (willpower) and pathways (waypower) to support and build up their faith in themselves. That faith acts as a cornerstone they use to form appraisals or beliefs to achieve the goals they set for themselves.[14] They see challenging goals as a regular part of daily life and, because of that, develop more goals. Having multiple goals during hard times gives a person alternate goals that can keep hope alive when one goal might be unreachable.

If a goal is the bullseye on a dartboard, the high-hope person sets out a large number of darts (pathways). They then use their agency (willpower) to throw dart after dart at the bullseye. With each throw, they increase their chance of hitting the goal. Should they miss the target and run out of darts (pathways), they look at some of the other targets/goals they have set for themselves. They begin throwing at that new bullseye goal but still remember the old goal. Should they hit the second target, they use their newly gained hope to return to the challenging goal/bullseye and keep trying. Setting multiple goals provides a way to constantly refill hope and decrease the anxiety mounting due to frustration. They use their hope to dismantle mounting worries and to clear their mind to ensure optimal brain functioning to hit the goal/target and improve learning.

Where does this leave those with low hope?

Do they set goals?

Do they believe in those goals?

Yes, they do, but the goals they create hold them back.

Those with low hope set fewer goals that are not as challenging. They have negative appraisals and believe that they most likely won't reach those goals. Negative appraisals also increase the chance of a person giving up on their goals when facing a challenge or setback. They don't invest as much in their goals because they don't believe they're attainable. Low-hope goal setting is a problem because it's one of the factors that can damage a child's future.

Goals set the course for what we are capable of becoming. Your life is a journey to various goal destinations: a new job, a better mindset, being the first person in your family to graduate college. When we take the journey to reach a goal, it's easy to get lost, confused, and frustrated. When a barrier appears in our path, the hope you have inside pushes you to keep going, find a way around it, dig under it, throw your resources and tools over the wall—commit to finding

FIGURE 3.6 GOALS AND HOPE LEVELS

THE IMPACT OF HOPE ON GOAL SETTING

LOW HOPE SCORE	MODERATE HOPE SCORE	HIGH HOPE SCORE
• Have few or no goals for different areas of their life.	• Have a few goals for different areas of their life.	• Have several goals for different areas of their life.
• Take on easy smaller goals and challenges.	• Take on easy to medium goals and challenges.	• Take on some of the most difficult goals and challenges.
• Have an appraisal that they most likely will not achieve their goals.	• Have an appraisal that they might achieve their goals.	• Have an appraisal that they WILL achieve their goals.

SOURCE: Adapted from Cheavens, J. S., Heiy, J. E., Feldman, D. B., Benitez, C., & Rand, K. L. (2018). Hope, goals, and pathways: Further validating the hope scale with observer ratings. *The Journal of Positive Psychology, 14*(4), 452–462. https://doi.org/10.1080/17439760.2018.1484937

a way no matter what. Thomas Edison did it when he publicly announced he would create light but didn't yet know how. Martin Luther King Jr. did it when he committed to showcasing his goals in speech form. These men let their hope focus their thoughts, attention, and resources on finding a way to their goal. They didn't have the answers initially, but hope gave them the courage to keep going and keep growing. The goal isn't what causes growth. The journey does.

> The goal isn't what causes growth. The journey does.

If a person has low hope, the journey to achieving goals is often cut short when barriers appear. If someone has little agency and few pathways, barriers appear bigger and more menacing, often causing those with low hope to avoid them, give up, or take on less challenging goals. They miss meaningful opportunities to stretch, push, and test their limits. You see, it's not about the goal as much as it's about learning what strengths and character traits hide within a person. Through goals, a person learns what they are capable of, and from that, they grow and discover deep reserves of determination, talents, and strengths they can use throughout their life. That's why goal setting is a foundational part of increasing hope and life outcomes for students.

The Learning Goal Cycle

Together with a safe environment and asset-based relationships (discussed in Chapter 2), goal setting can provide a vast amount of hope. Research on the connection between student-teacher relationships and students' psychological well-being found that in the context of a safe, supportive relationship with a teacher, students may acquire more confidence in their own abilities.[15] Confidence and continual support allow a mental shift to occur in which student problems can go from overwhelming to a welcome challenge. This shift fosters hope and positive attributions and ultimately motivates students to achieve their goals. That's why goal setting to increase hope should start in the classroom, with the teacher. A great way to get students to utilize goal setting is using the learning goal cycle.

The learning goal cycle utilizes the concept of goal stretching to build hope. Goal stretching is a concept Dr. Rick Snyder, the founder of hope psychology, recommends in his book *The Psychology of Hope*. Goal stretching involves students setting and organizing goals based on previous performance and sets them up for success because the goals are slightly above their current level. It's called a "stretch" goal because it stretches their abilities, learning, and strengths to a new level. To apply goal stretching daily, I created the learning goal cycle. The cycle uses student feedback and a learner's progress to help students set, organize, and monitor learning goals. Not only does it increase hope but it aids students in improving their mastery of classroom concepts.

You will notice on the hopeful start flowchart that feedback happens after every lesson or activity. You may not have the time to provide daily feedback, but allowing students at least one opportunity a week to take their work to a partner to get feedback for the learning goal cycle is invaluable. The students with partners or hope mentors can set academic goals through giving and receiving feedback. Feedback provides students with a way to focus their efforts and improve results.

Feedback provides students with a way to focus their efforts and improve results.

It also serves to promote goal setting. The learning goal cycle allows students to see their strengths and use them to work on their weaknesses.

At the end of an assignment, activity, or project, the partners give a glow and grow on each other's work. A *glow* is one specific strength that is visible in the work they're critiquing. One of the partners takes the strength and the knowledge from the lesson to explain why the other partner's work was effective. A *grow* is a helpful suggestion to improve the work. The glow/grow model works best when it is taught explicitly to students early in the year. That way, they understand what their feedback should look like. Students of any age can learn to critique the work of others. A feedback tip sheet works well to provide students with a guide to giving glows and grows to partners.

The tip sheet guides students through the steps to take when giving a glow and a grow. It also offers sentence frames students can use to build their feedback. The best way to ensure students give quality feedback is by practicing. For example, I ask a student volunteer to pretend to be my partner and use a generic example assignment for the model. I explain aloud how I create the glow/grow feedback

FIGURE 3.7   TIPS FOR FEEDBACK

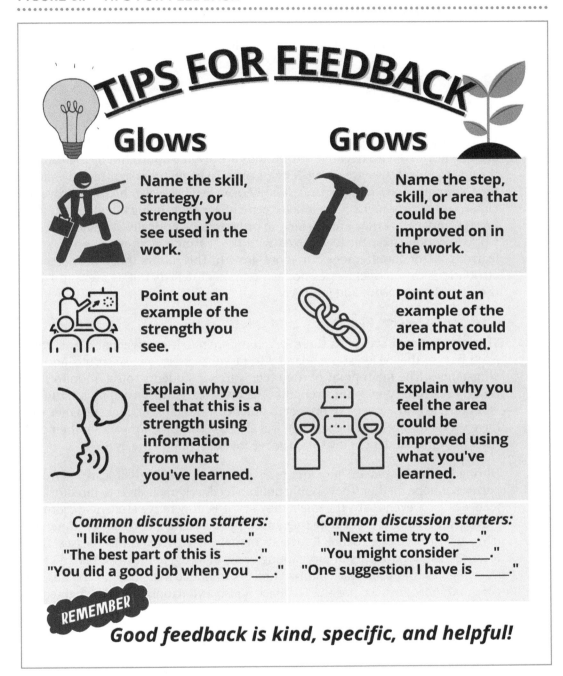

using the tip sheet as a guide. Once I finish, the students check if my feedback is kind, helpful, and specific. It's fun to throw in a bad example so that they can catch an error in the feedback to know what not to do.

After the model, students practice glow/grow feedback in pairs using a previous assignment. They write down their feedback as they go through the work, giving each other glows and grows. I use their recorded glows/grows to provide additional ways they can improve their critique. Once all students give a successful glow and grow, I use glow/grow feedback with all work. That's why it is a check-out for the end of activities or lessons on the hopeful start flowchart. Feedback gives a person a chance to improve and set goals using the learning goal cycle.

> Feedback gives a person a chance to improve and set goals using the learning goal cycle.

When students see a piece of work, experience with feedback teaches them to critique it. Those with negative attributions are given a mind shift by focusing on the good in what they are doing. It helps them to begin to recognize and validate their strengths, providing balance. Glow/grow feedback also helps improve the classroom environment. First, it helps cement concepts being taught as students have to apply what they are learning in order to look critically at someone else's work. Secondly, peer feedback used with the learning goal cycle conveys that learning is not about grades but about growth. This allows those with negative attributions to see weaknesses not as permanent deficits but as areas in which they can change, grow, and improve.

The Cycle: Learn, Feedback, and Goals

The learning goal cycle has three key components: learn, feedback, and goals. Each part of the cycle can be adapted to fit your classroom, schedule, and circumstances. The main point of the cycle is to get students to set, monitor, and reflect on stretch goals and strengths. The cycle starts with learning as students work on a lesson, activity, or project to practice a standard or concept. Once they have set their first stretch goal, they will also use this time to work on their goal. After learning, students move into the feedback section of the cycle.

During feedback, students give and receive glows/grows on their learning from a partner or hope mentor. They should utilize a feedback track sheet to monitor their feedback and, eventually, the goals they set. It is imperative students record the glow/grow feedback every time they meet. By recording feedback over time, students have the chance to look for trends in their strengths and weaknesses. Grow feedback assists students in pinpointing areas of struggle they can use to create stretch goals. Glow feedback allows students to notice their unique abilities, talents, and skills. Focused positive feedback is also a vital tool for future goal setting.

> By recording feedback over time, students have the chance to look for trends in their strengths and weaknesses.

Many schools focus on having students set goals by making educational decisions on future career paths. Frequently students guess at what they like and build a goal from the guess. This process is mixed up. Students shouldn't have to mold themselves to fit a job. This is not a stretch of their abilities or talents, it's a guess. Students need the opportunity to recognize their unique skills and to use those skills to plan immediate, long-term, and life goals. Consistent glow/grow

FIGURE 3.8   LEARNING GOAL CYCLE

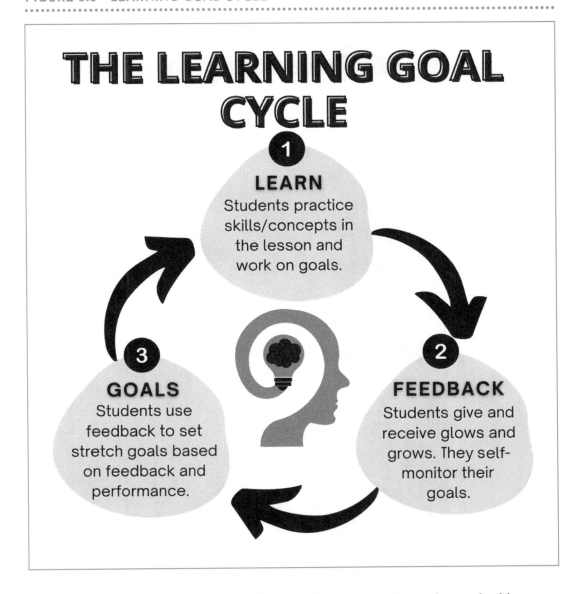

feedback focuses students on using what they learn about themselves to build goals for a future they'll love and enjoy.

After students receive feedback, they move into goal setting. There are two types of goals students can utilize: immediate and stretch goals. Immediate goals are set when students take action on a grow by applying the feedback to their work right away. A student could set an immediate goal if they feel they could fix the issue quickly; for instance, they forgot a step in a math problem, didn't write a conclusion on a paper, left out a hypothesis in their lab work, or spelled a prominent historical figure's name wrong. For an immediate goal, the student applies the grow feedback right away by revising their work using the feedback or applying the feedback the next day.

FIGURE 3.9 FEEDBACK TRACKING FORM

Name: _____ Partner's name: _____ Start date: _____ End date: _____

The goal I am working on is: _____

WHAT WAS THE ACTIVITY, LESSON, OR PROJECT?	GLOW WHAT STRENGTH IS IN YOUR WORK? HOW COULD YOU USE THIS TO HELP YOUR GROW SECTION?	GROW APPLY THE GROW! REVISE AND FIX THE WORK, OR USE THE FEEDBACK AND APPLY IT TOMORROW.	GOAL TRACKING TALK TO YOUR PARTNER ABOUT YOUR GOAL AND WHERE YOU ARE IN YOUR PLAN. REVISE THE GOAL IF NECESSARY.

Weekly stretch goal: Do you need more time on a goal? Was anything hard for you this week? Did you notice any patterns in your grow feedback this week? Is there an area, skill, or strategy you need more help or practice with? Set a SMART goal (**s**pecific, **m**easurable, **a**chievable, **r**elevant, and **t**ime-bound).

_____

_____

_____

_____

There are two types of goals students can utilize: immediate and stretch goals.

Students self-monitor their short-term goals. For example, if a student forgot to carry a number, it would be recorded as an immediate goal in the area of goal tracking. Going forward, the student would self-monitor to avoid making the same mistake that led to the goal. A student can see if the immediate goal worked to fix the weakness by tracking feedback and performance. Should the weakness become a roadblock, the immediate goal can turn into a stretch goal.

Goals are set weekly or biweekly to allow students to collect a substantial amount of feedback/evidence to analyze. During the goal-setting section of the learning goal cycle, students work with their partner or independently to reflect on their performance using feedback and work to create a stretch goal. Students should use the acronym SMART to make sure the goal they set is structured for success (the goal should be specific, measurable, achievable, relevant, and time-bound). The first few times students set goals, they may need help building a SMART stretch goal. You could help them by doing a whole group lesson and walking students through the parts of a SMART goal to create their first stretch goal. After the initial lesson, give students a SMART goal guide sheet to remind them of the process.

Students then move back into the learn phase, where they continue to practice content and work to achieve their stretch goal. After they receive glow and grow feedback for the day, they record the feedback along with a reflection in their goal progress column. At the end of the weekly or biweekly period, students move back into the goal phase to assess progress on the goal they set for themselves and create new goals. If they met the goal, they use their feedback tracking sheet and materials from the week to set a new goal. However, if they did not meet their goal, students can modify the goal. The student can extend their stretch goal if they need more time, change the stretch goal to make it more attainable, get help to set a new goal to address roadblocks, or use chunking to break down the goal into smaller pieces. Whether they modify an existing goal or move on to a new goal, the cycle begins again.

The learning goal cycle fosters hope as students problem-solve ways to achieve their goals (pathways). They gain willpower as they build on previous success (agency). By accomplishing stretch goals, students learn to welcome more complex challenges (goals). Plus, the noticeable success students achieve assists those with low hope to stay engaged in their journey to build more hope. It's a simple hope practice that fits with any grade and curriculum.

By accomplishing stretch goals, students learn to welcome more complex challenges (goals).

With every student focused on personal growth, every child can experience success. This is critical as education is often caught up with comparisons. What's the norm? Highest GPA? Who is the best? With a comparison focus, a child sees education as a race that some are already winning, discouraging them from even

FIGURE 3.10   BUILDING A SMART GOAL

When writing SMARTgoals, be specific! These steps are designed to help you succeed, so be positive and try your best to find a way to fulfill each one. Remember, if you get stuck on a step, you can get help from your partner, from your teacher, or from classroom materials or the Internet.

INITIAL GOAL	Write the goal you have in mind.
S **SPECIFIC**	What do you want to accomplish? Who needs to be included? When do you want to do this? Why is this a goal?
M **MEASURABLE**	How can you measure progress and know if you've successfully met your goal?
A **ACHIEVABLE**	Do you have the skills required to reach your goal? If not, can you find a way to get them or learn them? What is the motivation for this goal? Is the amount of effort required worth what the goal will achieve?
R **RELEVANT**	Why am I setting this goal now? Is it aligned with the person I want to be?
T **TIME-BOUND**	What's the deadline to accomplish this goal, and is it realistic?

SMART goal: Review what you have written and craft a new goal statement using all the answers to the questions above.

starting. Comparing and ranking doesn't provide information to strengthen and improve performance.

Recent studies in psychology show that goals centered around comparison hurt memory.[16] For example, if you tell a child to try to beat the class average on a project, they will set a goal in comparison to their peers. The goal will cause them to focus on comparing themselves with other students, and it will impact their ability to form memories around their learning. Plus, they will face more stress as they measure their success in comparison to their peers. Allowing students to set achievement goals based on their drive to master something is better for memory and values individual progress.

> Allowing students to set achievement goals based on their drive to master something is better for memory and values individual progress.

The learning goal cycle works to alleviate this comparison anxiety as students focus on their own paths. This cycle teaches students that comparison isn't important. It reinforces that it's okay just to be yourself. The cycle puts the student in the driver's seat of their learning as they use goals, pathways, and agency to improve themselves. Students see their growth. Their growth grows their confidence. Their confidence grows their hope. The cycle repeats over and over, sending a clear message to students that they are worthy, they matter, and their growth is important.

FIGURE 3.11 GOALS DO'S AND DON'TS

Goals to Increase 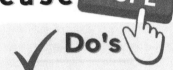 HOPE

 **Don'ts**

- **Don't** rush a student when they are selecting a goal.
- **Don't** assume all students can identify and develop plans to achieve their goals without support.
- **Don't** encourage a student to set a goal that is vastly outside their past performance levels.
- **Don't** overwhelm students by having them take on too many goals outside their comfort zone.
- **Don't** skim over goal setting. Time for goal setting/monitoring should be prioritized to help hope bloom.

✓ Do's

- **Do** ask about and show interest in students goals.
- **Do** listen and learn about students desires to help them carefully set goals that align with what they want.
- **Do** instruct students to make stretch goals that build on previous performance.
- **Do** help students to use their talents and strengths to reach their future goals.
- **Do** help students if they have conflicting goals. Show how this can be a problem and help them prioritize goals that matter.

HEART TO HEART

QUESTIONS AND IDEAS FOR ACTION

Reflect, discuss with a group, or share your thoughts and create a dialogue on social media using the book's hashtag, #HOPEforEdu.

Questions

1. Think of a time you were truly stuck on a goal or activity. What did you do to keep going? What do you do to combat internal and external barriers that might prevent you from reaching a goal? How can you use that knowledge to help your students?

2. Reflect on a previously achieved goal or accomplishment. What did reaching that goal or achievement teach you about yourself? How can goal setting help students to learn about themselves and build self-esteem?

3. Think about a time you were given specific feedback on something you did well. How did it make you feel, and how did it affect how you felt about the person who provided the feedback? How do you think giving feedback and reflecting on strengths daily will impact student perception of the classroom? How might it impact classroom culture?

Ideas for Action

- As students accomplish goals and build a list of glows, consider creating a wall of success. A wall of success works to help learners feel represented in the classroom, motivate them, and remind them of how far they have come. Use any area and create a square or rectangle section for each student labeled with their name. Allow students to post to the wall after they accomplish a goal or when they receive glow feedback they find impactful. This gives every child a chance to be represented in the classroom and highlights their work and talents. Plus, a wall of success can act as a pick-me-up for students to look at when they need the motivation to keep going.

- Have students plan rewards they would want to give themselves as they hit milestones to bigger stretch goals. Examples could be posting their success on the success wall, looking up funny jokes, watching a short inspirational speech or TED Talk, drawing a picture, writing a list of why they're awesome, or printing an image of something they love. The important part is to help students plan mini-rewards they can collect for making progress.

Once a student creates their rewards list, they can use it to keep their motivation up while working towards bigger stretch goals. A research study from 2018 titled *It's about Time: Earlier Rewards Increase Intrinsic Motivation* shows that having a person offer themselves an immediate reward during a more extended task strengthens the association between the activity and the goal of the activity, making a person feel like a task is rewarding in and of itself.[17] Immediate rewards increase the positive experience of the task, which improves outcomes for motivation and persistence.

Compassion for Colleagues

Overcoming: Growing Hopeful Cultures for the Long Game

In education, we often become stuck playing the short game. We develop tunnel vision because of day-to-day problems with "lack of." Lack of tissues. Lack of funds. Lack of help. We neglect our own hope and the long game or purpose by putting so much focus on the here and now. My daughter Bella once fell victim to short-game tunnel vision in a soccer game against a rival team.

Bella was new to the game and was preoccupied with getting the ball and managing her footing. Intently she watched her feet move the ball back and forth. The ball cut smoothly down the field as she passed it from foot to foot. Then calamity struck. Her focus was so fixed on the ball that she missed the group of rival players who encircled her like sharks on the field. They crept in, and with her focus stuck on the ball, she fell victim to an ambush. They swooped in and overwhelmed her. Inches from the goal, they stole the ball. Bella was left baffled and upset at her missed opportunity.

What Bella did wasn't wrong. Bella needed to have some focus on the here and now. She was new to the game, as some of your staff may be. All she wanted was to learn the basics well, but because she became so focused on only the small details, she missed the big one: the goal. This also happens in schools. School staff can become so focused on fixing everyday problems that personal growth, self-care, and engagement with the job decline because they miss the goal.

> School staff can become so focused on fixing everyday problems that personal growth, self-care, and engagement with the job decline because they miss the goal.

Hope Matters

The goal for staff is not just to support and educate students but to be models of learning and support for each other. That starts at the top with being models for both learning *and* hope as well. Like students, the long game of education isn't filling heads with content; it's helping someone discover and fulfill their potential. School staff who become fixated on problems often forget and neglect their own potential to deal with today's problems.

That personal neglect can have ripple effects. According to recent Gallup research, 67 percent of U.S. employees are disengaged from work.[1] Engagement might not seem like a big deal until you look at the definition they use for engagement, which is "the extent an employee feels passionate and committed to an organization and their work."[2] It's the level of care a person has for the work they are doing. If we have school staff who become disengaged and only see short-game problems, it will create ripple effects in the building, such as staff members doing the bare minimum to get by, colleagues getting burned out, and people quitting. Students witness models of disengagement and disengage themselves. It's a perfect storm of how cultures can influence the environment. The key to school culture and growth has been and always will be the hope of the workforce.

Measuring and growing hope in school staff can change school culture and create an environment that supports growth, happiness, and fulfillment for every person in the building. This isn't a one-day practice; it's a mind shift to daily living, breathing, and increasing hope and engagement. A research study on hope's impact in the workplace found that hope works to enhance job engagement and workplace outcomes.[3] The more hope a worker has, the more they care about their work. The higher the hope level, the greater the faith and belief an employee has in their place of employment.

Hope affects our mood, our environment, and, most importantly, the colleagues and students we come in contact with. The level of hope a person brings to the table contributes to the hope an organization transmits to others. If employees are low in hope, the organization can become low in hope. The more we work to improve our own hope levels, the more we can improve the hope levels for every person who walks in the building. Think about a moment where you felt truly accomplished. Perhaps the day you graduated or got a degree? Maybe when you learned to drive? Or the day you did something difficult? How did you feel? Now take it one step further and think of the people you interacted with that day. Think about their body language: How did they seem to look and feel? Our emotions are contagious, and the more hope we have in the building, the more of a positive emotional force we will have driving our school culture.[4]

> Hope affects our mood, our environment, and, most importantly, the colleagues and students we come in contact with.

Hope is a pivotal part of the engagement equation, and engagement drives performance. Someone who feels that they matter, that they are supported, and that their well-being is being cared for will do more and become more. They are not going to turn around and leave an organization. Hope is a long-game strategy that, when implemented, can work to attract and retain staff to school buildings. The long-game goal is to support the growth of every team member, building up their potential, and that starts with hope.

> Hope is a pivotal part of the engagement equation, and engagement drives performance.

Leadership Teams Matter

Just as teachers build hope for students, leaders need to develop and measure hope for school staff. Measuring hope for school staff can be done using the Adult Hope Scale on page 51. Results are compiled similarly to the Children's Hope Scale. Each staff member will end up with two subscores for pathways and agency and one overall hope score. Once leaders know the hope score for individual employees, they can begin to support rising hope in the building and with it employee job satisfaction and engagement.

This test can help with school culture in multiple ways. First, taking the time to measure hope levels provides a snapshot of the hope in the building. It helps a leader know if the psychological needs of the staff are being met and can point to areas where hope may be lacking. Measuring hope throughout the year can also point leaders to employees who may be struggling and need some extra support. Sometimes people become so self-reliant they don't want to share their problems, and this test allows a person the anonymity to keep their problem to themself but still get support. It can also serve to help check on how the staff is doing after the implementation of new practices or school-wide initiatives. Making sure staff are doing and feeling okay after a major shift can help leaders better support staff members.

This test could also be used in the recruiting of new staff members. Frequently we look at a person's resume and guess how they might fit into a work environment. Hope scores can help leaders purposefully choose an individual with higher hope, ensuring the employee has the resilience and flexibility to do well in a new position and help the organization thrive.[5] It's a great tool that could be used to whittle down candidates so schools purposefully hire individuals who will bring with them psychological capital that will add to the school culture.

Hiring high-hope people will increase engagement, but raising hope in current school staff can do the same. Staff members with low hope scores need extra support to grow their scores and with this find more satisfaction in the workplace. Much like I pair students off with hope mentors, school staff should be provided opportunities to work and strengthen their hope by interacting with higher-hope staff models. It's important to provide the built-in support of hopeful models to balance out the daily dealings of the short game and the long game of the growth of the staff. Without built-in support it will be easy for staff to get overwhelmed and lose heart if they have nothing to drive them and support them to keep going.

> School staff should be provided opportunities to work and strengthen their hope by interacting with higher-hope staff models.

I had a colleague, let's call her Mary, who might have left teaching if it wasn't for a shift in support of her hope. Mary was a new teacher in one of the first buildings I worked in. She struggled with keeping up her own hope and surviving her first year. Mary was paired with another new teacher and did not have a lot of opportunities to get support from higher-hope models. Mary had difficulty with grading and managing her time, but she told no one. She had to take on a second job when she experienced car problems, but again no one knew she was burning the candle at both ends. She didn't want to bother anyone, so her classroom struggled as she suffered in silence.

A monthly mentor check-in was simple, with Mary reporting things were A-OK, but the reality was her hope and health had begun to take a nosedive. When it came time for her to fill out her intent form, she wrote, "I'm going to quit." My principal called me into her office and asked me to check on Mary.

I met with her on the weekend just to talk. She told me that she just couldn't manage everything. She said her year had been a struggle and having to work with another new teacher was like the blind leading the blind. All she wanted was some support. I asked my principal to switch her to the grade level I worked on so she could be around some veteran educators with high hope. Mary reconsidered leaving when I told her I would work with her to find ways to help her manage. Mary loved technology and wanted to find ways to use more technology to manage her workload.

The next year the new grade-level team worked to make sure Mary had time to go and observe others, and we met weekly to share ideas for lessons. Toward the end of the second year, Mary started setting goals to get Google-certified to strengthen her skills. I worked with her to get certified as well. We met and went through the online training programs together. At the end of the year, Mary passed the Google level one certification test and gained more tools for grading management. The first year left her questioning her ability to teach, but after the support she received the second year, she found renewed hope and decided teaching really was her calling. It would have been easy to dismiss Mary, but our job isn't to try and catch staff members at their worst, it is to help build them up to their best. That's why this is a shift in mentality. We can't just abandon staff when they struggle, we need to work with them side by side to find ways to help them thrive.

Leaders can implement opportunities for school staff to feel supported and raise hope levels in staff in multiple ways. The critical component to raising hope with adults is that staff members are given numerous avenues to work on their hope and build relationships with higher-hope models.

Goals and Coaching

Every person can get better, and part of raising hope for school staff is giving them pathways to get there. Goal setting is fundamental for supporting the budding growth of hope. Hope is instilled as staff members meet goals and set new ones. The learning goal cycle from above supports staff goals and growth. To help staff members gain hope, growth goals have to become a focus. Many schools have teachers set a professional growth goal for the year. The problem with this is it only happens once, may be dictated by data or a test, and doesn't help the staff member focus on and find solutions for their problems or areas of weakness. Plus, it's individual, and there may be no one there to assist with the goal. The staff member is left on their own to succeed or fail, which isolates and disengages them.

Part of raising hope for school staff is giving them pathways to get there.

Instructional coaching can work with the learning goal cycle to support setting and reaching goals, aiding every person to grow and gain accomplishment. One of the ways to utilize this cycle is through partnered coaching. Staff should have options of people they could partner with for coaching when using the learning goal cycle. Partnering with a fellow school or another district to raise hope can offer you more options to help staff members that might be the only type of instructor in a school, such as a reading specialist. That way you open up the pool of hopeful mentors to a larger group and can gain ideas and tools from new cultures as you work together to monitor and strengthen hope. This creates a hope cohort that you can utilize to offer low-hope staff members options of a few higher-hope mentors they could use during the year. Staff can use the learning goal cycle to set goals relating to an area they are struggling with, a problem they are having, something new they want to try, something they want feedback on, or something they want to get even better at on the job.

The leadership component comes into play when leaders give staff the time and opportunity to utilize the cycle. This shows that the leadership in the building supports the goals and growth of the team. This may mean providing coverage for teachers, getting parent volunteers to cover duties, and/or working with staff to find ways to buy supplies and materials. It doesn't matter what it takes because the investment the leadership makes in the staff will always pay off in the improvement in culture that results.

Once a staff member has set a goal, they must have a partner as they start to work on their goal. The goal should be SMART, and staff could utilize the same goal-planning sheet students use to set stretch goals for themselves. Schools could do this once a day, week, month, or quarter, but it needs to be done often for staff to feel growth and raise hope. Doing this only once will not impact staff or make them feel supported; it will make it feel like it's a simple drive-by initiative. Hope is something that has to be built and maintained. Goals need to be set frequently to help people grow and keep hope levels high. If we don't work to focus school attention on increasing the potential of every employee, schools won't get better. This means *everyone*— secretaries, nurses, instructional assistants, custodial staff, teachers, technicians, librarians, administrators, and more—needs support to become stronger and better. By improving their potential, we improve our schools. This is important because when employees grow and get better, schools grow and get better.

Hope is something that has to be built and maintained.

After the partnered pair has shared their goals, each member of the pair should be given time to observe their partner's goal in action. This builds in personal accountability and support as staff members work to get better. Just as students give glow and grow feedback, staff partners should do the same, providing helpful, kind, supportive feedback on strengths and weaknesses they see that pertain to the goal. Staff can use this feedback to set new goals and gain a sense of accomplishment as they track and see their growth with each goal they attain. This is not just one more thing to add the plate of our staff members, it is a process that will relieve burdens and solve problems as they arise.

Staff members should be encouraged to choose a goal to work on, be given built-in time and support to work on the goal cycle, and, when they get stuck, be offered the support of a colleague to help them reach their goal. This does take up time and resources, but it creates supportive cultures that thrive and that radiate hope.

Learning Walks

Just as high-hope student mentors can model hope to low-hope students, high-hope staff can do the same through modeling in scheduled learning walks. Learning walks are an invaluable way to gain perspective on the ways high-hope models operate in their work environment. When leaders encourage staff to provide open opportunities to observe and get ideas from each other, staff can discover new pathways they can use in their work. Learning walks will look different for various staff positions and vary from job to job.

For example, teachers on staff should be encouraged to open their classrooms to fellow teachers to come and observe the classroom management and instructional practices they use for content and building hope. A simple way to do this is to ask some higher-hope educators to open their classrooms for a round of learning walks on a specific day. On the day of the learning walk, educators in the building are given a list of the high-hope teachers who have opted to open their classrooms. The teachers who want to participate could use their planning time or get coverage to go and watch.

The teacher observers should provide feedback by pointing out something they liked and one thing they learned or might want to try. They should take these thoughts with them to utilize on their own goal cycle journey. By allowing open access to higher-hope models and giving teachers the time to learn from other experts in the building, leaders can show they value the expertise and hope of their staff and support collegial observations and conversations on the strengths of others.

As the year progresses and teachers gain more hope, learning walks should open to the entire teaching staff to share their best lessons and trade secrets. It's essential that the walks start with high-hope models. Later, as low-hope staff members gain hope, they should become included as models. As more walks happen and showcase the strengths of the teaching staff, the pedagogy of the staff will get stronger.

The same holds true for other positions on staff. Instead of having an open learning walk, staff members with fewer comparable positions in the building should be given time to go and observe a high-hope colleague in a fellow school or in the hope cohort you create. For example, the school nurse might go and observe a colleague from a partnered neighboring school for a morning, or the school librarian might open her library for other librarians to come and observe new practices. Every member of staff needs the opportunity to see how other high-hope individuals are doing their jobs. This allows the expertise of the staff to be strengthened through both giving advice on practices to help others and gaining advice on practices that might enhance their own job. Every member of staff was hired because of their skills, and it's time that sharing and developing those skills becomes foundational practice.

Often the best professional development comes from observing the ideas and practices in the room next door. Learning walks and similar exercises show off the staff's strengths and allow lower-hope colleagues to see strong models to support growing hope. This helps every person gain new ideas, tools, and hope they can use in their jobs.

A Shared Goal of Growth

Successful cultures create and sustain hope by utilizing small, simple practices to act as beacons focusing on the long game of hope and growth. Encouraging staff to support and help each other reach goals shows your colleagues that it's okay to have a short game, but we need to remember the long game of focusing not just on the daily education and development of students but on that of our colleagues too.

The engagement and actions of staff members drive culture, and that culture can only thrive if the people are thriving first. Yes, you might be short on tissues still, but through goal setting, you might find new ways to teach algorithms, help students draft papers, or provide more support for a student struggling emotionally. It shifts staff focus so they remember the long game. By implementing the learning goal cycle, coaching, and learning walks, we provide assistance to our colleagues, reminding them to grow hope, to keep going, and, most importantly, to take the time to focus on the goal so they don't miss their shot.

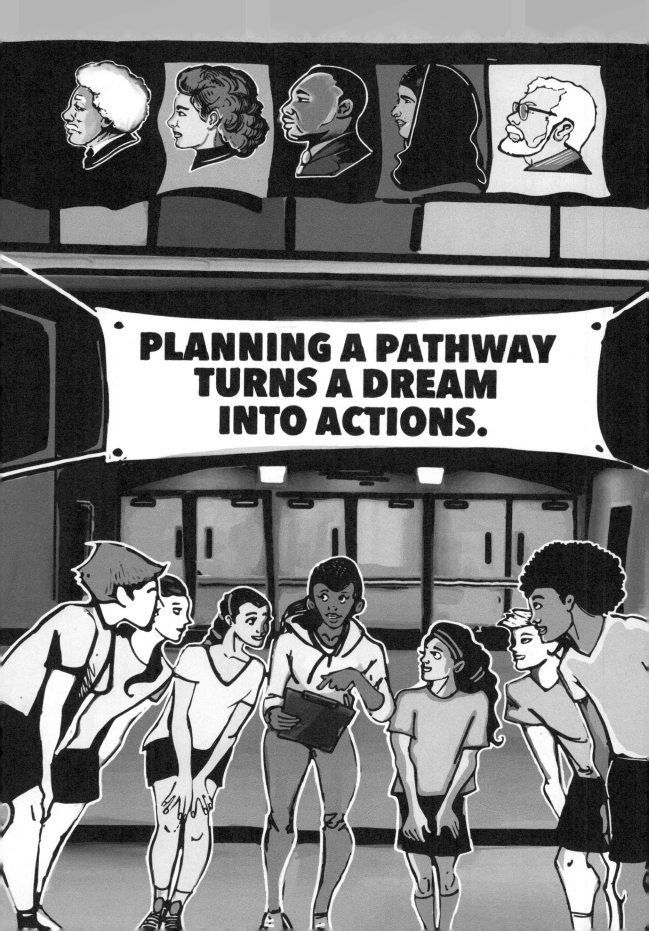

CHAPTER 4

PLANNING

Marco tapped his desk with his pencil as the school counselor walked the narrow aisle between groups of desks.

With cheerful enthusiasm, the counselor opened the coursebook for potential electives and said, "High school planning is where you can start to build a path to the person you want to become!"

Marco continued tapping his pencil on his desk. Leaning back in his chair, he slumped low as the counselor passed out scheduling documents. He scribbled a few notes on the coursebook in Spanish and sighed heavily, letting his dark hair cover his eyes.

I wandered closer to Marco's desk and knelt to his eye level. "Hey, Marco, you seem a bit tense. What's going on?"

Marco looked at me as the school counselor continued her presentation. He spoke low, trying not to disrupt her as she talked to the class. "My dad wants me to use my electives to take electrician classes so when I graduate, I can officially work with him."

I nodded and glanced at the electrical course description in the book in front of him, "That's a great way to learn about electrical components. Do you want to be an electrician?"

Marco answered, "All the men in my family are electricians and work in the family business."

I rephrased my question and tried again. "Wow, that sounds like a great tradition. So, you want to join the family business?"

Marco turned and started to fill out his schedule. "It's all my family does. My great grandfather brought the skill with him from Ecuador when he came to America, and it has provided my family with lots of security. I grew up knowing how to use a multimeter before I learned to read. I will be a great electrician because my family already taught me the basics. I go on jobs with my dad. I've already learned the skills I need."

I nodded. "So, your dream is to become an electrician?"

Marco leaned forward, intertwining his fingers as he pulled his arms tight around his chest. "It's what they want. I guess it's the only dream I've been allowed to have or think about. My dad says it's important to have security. We have always done this. It's a safe choice for my future. One where I won't be in debt or end up not finding a job. The world is crazy right now, so I guess I have to be an electrician."

As the school counselor walked to the other side of the room, I asked Marco, "If you could have your family's approval and support for your dream, what would you want to be?"

"I don't know. I guess I only ever saw being an electrician. I don't enjoy testing things, wiring things, and installing electrical drops. I guess I really don't like it, but jobs aren't supposed to be fun. My dad told me that jobs are meant to be a source of money. My dad hates his job, and at night he makes furniture to balance his day. Sometimes I help him with that too."

"So, your dad hates his job and comes home to do something fun to make his day feel better?"

Marco nodded and sat back. "Yep. I love my dad and my family. I just wish I could be me sometimes. Like this one time in seventh grade, I was pumped about my science project on cells. I built a plant cell from scraps around the house. It was awesome." He smiled, and his eyes seemed to dance as he continued talking.

"I loved making the plant cell and the microscopes the teacher let us use in class. I thought just for a second how cool it would be to just study things through a microscope. Later, I showed my dad the cell and told him all of the facts I learned. He looked happy until I told him I might want to study science and go to college to learn about things through a microscope. As soon as I told him, he looked mad and said science and college are not part of my reality.

"He told me college costs too much, and he doesn't make enough money to send me and raise my other brothers and sisters. Then my father said it was important for me to wake up to reality as he had never seen a Latino scientist. He told me no one like us ends up as scientists. I never really thought about it that way. I wanted to prove him wrong, but as I started flipping through my science stuff, I saw many old white guys and ladies and realized my dad was right: People like us are not scientists."

I could have offered Marco an encouraging word at that moment, but he needed more than encouragement. Cheerleading wouldn't help him believe his dream was possible. What he needed was to know that he could get to his goal. He needed a plan. So I grabbed some tools to help Marco, because when we don't believe something is possible, we lose hope, and without hope, we can develop possibility blindness.

POSSIBILITY BLINDNESS, PATHWAYS, AND LEARNING

Possibility blindness happens when a person develops an inability to see a future beyond the problems and reality of the current moment. Students with low pathways scores on the Children's Hope Scale or who score low on their perceived ability to plan routes to achieve their goals are very susceptible to possibility blindness. When a person with low pathway scores has tried a way around a problem that failed or can't readily find a solution, they limit what they think they can achieve. Marco, for example, was challenged by his family's belief that his dream was not realistic. Instead of trying to find different ways to address the problems his family presented, he accepted his family's belief and decided his only hope was to study science as a hobby.

> Possibility blindness happens when a person develops an inability to see a future beyond the problems and reality of the current moment.

With possibility blindness, a person can get bound in a cycle of accepting and never striving past the limitations of the present moment. Possibility blindness can obstruct a person's future and their ability to learn. Educational psychologist Lev Vygotsky indicated a sweet spot in which learning occurs called the zone of proximal development (ZPD). This zone occurs when students step out of what they know and are challenged to develop a new skill or understanding. The more time in the ZPD, the more a student learns and grows.

The ZPD is where a person begins to grasp an understanding of themself, their abilities, and their talents. The ZPD is a space where personality and identity are formed and restructured. It's where we stretch our potential.[1] A person's pathways and overall hope score tremendously impact what goes on in the ZPD.

Those with higher hope and pathways scores will strive to seek out and enter the ZPD more often and more readily. Why? They believe in their ability to find ways around barriers. In essence, a person with high pathways will find ways to push past their current limits and will even risk failure because they see failure as simply learning one path doesn't work on the way to a goal. Entering the ZPD doesn't mean that they will become masters of all subjects or all content. They enter the ZPD to discover new ways to adapt their strengths to the challenges they face.

Those with low hope and pathway scores will not actively seek to enter the ZPD because it's a place where they know they will face difficulties. It's not that they don't want to learn; it's that they often get stuck in the struggle and give up when they come to a problem. Those with low pathways need help, but we have to be careful of the help we give.

Sometimes we want to stop students from struggling by giving solutions or solving their issues. The problem with this is that if we do it and they get past their roadblock, they might expect others to solve their problems again in the future. We don't want to be the go-to for those with low pathways, and we don't help students by spoon-feeding knowledge. When students with low pathways struggle, we should respond by assisting them to problem-solve and generate new ways to tackle problems, because the struggle is necessary.

> When students with low pathways struggle, we should respond by assisting them to problem-solve and generate new ways to tackle problems, because the struggle is necessary.

PRODUCTIVE VS. DESTRUCTIVE STRUGGLE

Productive struggle is part of deep learning and allows students to develop neural pathways and cement learning. When we learn something, knowledge enters our brain like a car being plopped down in the middle of a field. The new knowledge must work to make a connection or path between neurons in the brain. The only problem? There is no road. The car must struggle through the field grass like our minds struggle to connect neurons. The car may hit a rock or get a flat tire on the path to get where it needs to go. The action we take in a student's moment of struggle influences how they perceive and approach struggle.

We can foster and support productive struggle by offering redos and retakes for learning targets, giving specific feedback, and allowing students time to reflect and break through their barriers. However, there is a thin line between productive and destructive struggle. Destructive struggle replaces productive struggle when a student feels unsupported and abandoned and believes that learning is impossible. We foster destructive struggle when we press on with material, set ambiguous learning targets, or give answers showing kids the struggle isn't worth it. The reason destructive struggle is so harmful is that when we don't allow new knowledge to push through and connect neurons, we don't allow a road to form. We might think we saved the student from struggle or hurt, but the reality is we hurt the student more by not letting them build a path for the knowledge in their mind.

As new knowledge struggles forward, it makes a rough road neurons can use to connect. All that effort and struggle gets noticed by our magnificent minds. The brain, wanting to conserve resources and energy, sends construction workers known as glial cells to the scene. The glial cells take stock of all the energy we spend trying to drive the new knowledge car from neuron to neuron. The brain doesn't want to waste energy, so the glial cells decide to build a road of myelin using the worn path. The initial, superficial learning of the car's path gets

FIGURE 4.1 DESTRUCTIVE VS. PRODUCTIVE

FOSTERING PRODUCTIVE vs. DESTRUCTIVE LEARNING STRUGGLE

PRODUCTIVE	DESTRUCTIVE
Feedback provides students with concrete action steps, strategies, or new resources for practice/relearning of material.	Feedback is generic, or questions are marked right or wrong with no action steps or guidance for the student.
There are clear learning targets. Students have rubrics or specific success criteria to gauge when they have mastered a skill or learning goal.	The skill or learning goal is ambiguous. Students practice and work on the skill with no concept of when they have met mastery.
The student is given opportunitites to redo assignments, reassess, and revisit skills as learning progresses throughout the year.	The student has limited opportunity for mastery. Class learning is centered on pacing guides or when a specific number of students reach mastery.
Students are given time to reflect, collaborate, problem-solve, and set goals for classroom learning targets or skills.	Students are expected to remember the material and build on concepts regardless of their level of understanding.

transformed into deep learning–learning that sticks, is remembered, and that can be utilized and accessed easily. The way we respond to struggle determines the depth of student learning.

Supporting productive struggle allows students to delve deep into learning and develop perseverance and grit. Psychologist Angela Duckworth has written extensively on grit and how it correlates to a person's future success. She studied multiple successful youths and found grit is key to students reaching more significant goals. Duckworth defines *grit* as "passion and perseverance for long-term goals."[2] Through building hope and pathways, we fuel kids' belief in themselves, their goals, and their ability to achieve their goals. Hope fuels grit, and grit gets kids past the struggles and trials of life. We have to develop hope so students can develop grit.

Grit is key to students reaching more significant goals.

The development of grit isn't easy. One of the hardest things I have had to do as a parent is watch my children struggle as they plan and reach for goals. My kids went through so much trauma before they came to live with us, so I wanted to protect them from struggle; I was worried that it would cause more trauma. At first, I tried to safeguard them. My children had missed a lot of early schooling due to abuse and moves between multiple foster families. Their spotty school attendance left gaps in their learning, especially for my older children.

The first time my oldest son brought home homework, he sat at our dining room table after dinner working on one paper for three hours. I checked in on him and offered to help, but he insisted on doing it alone. By the time he told me he was done, it was bedtime. He was beaming because he had done it, and despite having spent a long time on it, he bounced to the bedroom proud of his work.

I was proud of his work too, until I started putting away his paper. When I looked at the paper he had toiled away on, I realized he had only done the front page. He forgot the back. Not only that, but the math word problems he did on the front were wrong. I didn't want to tell him and take away the feeling of accomplishment, so I did a horrible thing: I corrected it and wrote all the answers.

The next day he came home humming. As he sat eating his snack, I found the homework paper stuffed deep in his backpack. He got a 98 percent, missing just one problem. The guilt overwhelmed me, and I had to confess what I had done. I said, "Son, I did something wrong. I didn't want to make you feel bad after you worked so hard on your homework last night, so I fixed it."

He patted my hand. "I already knew that, Mom. As soon as I went to turn my paper in, I knew. I don't write neat and straight like that."

"You knew? Why didn't you say something?"

"I told my teacher that I didn't understand the math after she graded the paper. I didn't want that grade because it felt bad, like having someone else run a race. She was confused because I only missed one. That's when I told her someone else filled it in.

"My teacher thanked me for my honesty and gave me some math videos and games to practice the new problems. I worked with her at school to redo the problems on a new paper. I hid the old paper in my backpack. If it took me a couple of hours, you probably worked hard! I didn't want you to feel bad that you are big and missed kid math problems. But now that you found it, the good news is I have some math videos we can watch to get better."

At that moment, my son reminded me why productive struggle is important: so that we can get better. Each struggle we overcome gives us hope and belief in ourselves. Without grit, hope, and pathways, students will avoid trying or quit when they struggle. We can't truly learn if we settle for only what we can do right now and never attempt to push past limits, barriers, and our current understanding. Oh, we can memorize, regurgitate facts, show steps in a problem, but we don't learn what is most important. The real learning of the ZPD is discovering the innate potential, strengths, and resilience each of us harbors inside.

AVOIDING CHALLENGE

Giving up in the ZPD is a problem, but if someone avoids challenges altogether they limit what they will become. Just because Marco's parents had never seen someone who looked like them go into a science-related field, they thought the possibility of this dream succeeding was slim to none.

They wanted what was best for their child, and because his dream seemed as fantastical to them as sprouting wings and flying, they tried to bring in a sense of reality to help him choose a safer, more realistic path. Marco's parents were not trying to be mean—they were trying to ensure he found a successful future. The only problem is that by pushing Marco not to test his strengths or skills in science, they were keeping him from discovering the depth of his passion or talent.

Goals that push us and time problem-solving in the ZPD are critical for forging a successful, fulfilling future. The goals that make up our pathways help us get to where we want to go. However, it's equally essential that the goal is a place we desire to go! There is no point in planning a path if it leads to nowhere or to a place you hate because then you'll avoid the goal.

Marco avoided listing classes on his course manual. He knew the class he needed to take—the course number was right in front of him. But he didn't want that goal and he didn't want to take the path, and so he dragged his feet, hoping to keep some distance between himself and the plan to become an electrician. The father of hope theory, Dr. Rick Snyder, defined pathway planning as "the human ability to generate different ways from the present to a desired future."[3] In that definition, a person's hope pathway is broken down into two components: making a path and envisioning a desired destination.

> A person's hope pathway is broken down into two components: making a path and envisioning a desired destination.

The future gives us strength and motivation to deal with problems and challenges while we forge a path to our dreams. Belief in a desired future creates momentum for the way we take. A desire mixed with belief in achieving a future is the energy of our hope. Without passion and desire for the future, we lack the power to move and tackle our dreams.

We will not dedicate ourselves to a planned pathway if the end goal is not worth it or if we believe a dream or goal is impossible. Beliefs can prevent us from taking steps to the future we desire before we even start. Marco enjoyed science and thought studying science would be a possible career option. However, once his family showed him their belief structure, he shut down the possibility of envisioning a future outside of being an electrician. Ultimately, the beliefs we hold fuel or deplete our hope pathways.

Building Confidence and Pathways

One way to help students like Marco reignite belief in their ability is to increase their confidence. In the last chapter, I mentioned the importance of glows, or positive feedback, in goal pursuit. That feedback becomes even more crucial when students must build new pathways to handle a problem. The glows a student collects while working on class content or academic goals can boost confidence and create new ideas for pathway formation.

Sometimes we simply forget what we're good at or isolate that attribute to a single part of our life. By having students list their strengths when facing a problem, you remind them of a piece of themselves that makes them feel confident, and this can help them think of new ways to utilize their strengths. This process also helps students develop new, personalized ways of learning, which increases divergent thinking and creativity in the classroom.

When a student initially becomes stuck, I provide them with the building new pathways organizer seen in Figure 4.2 to help break down the problem. The student first lists specific details of their stuck point. Once they feel they have identified the problem, they move on to take stock of their strengths and of resources at their disposal. Taking stock of resources helps the student shift their focus from being problem oriented to solution oriented.

> Taking stock of resources helps the student shift their focus from being problem oriented to solution oriented.

The most important part of this graphic organizer is connecting how the strengths and resources could be used to tackle the problem. The third column on the organizer is where the students increase their creativity and generate multiple paths for their situation. Students should try to create multiple possible solutions or next steps to address their issue in the pathways column. The key is not stopping after making only one pathway. When I initially model this activity with students, I point out that generating ideas in the third box is like buying a lottery ticket. If a person buys one ticket or takes one path, their chances of winning or solving the problem are low, but imagine if they purchased four, five, or even a thousand tickets. What happens then to their odds of success? They go up. The more pathways we form, the greater chance a person can successfully get past barriers to their goal.

I used the new pathways organizer with Marco. Under the problem section, he wrote out that he couldn't picture himself succeeding in science and thought his family's views were correct. He also listed that it was his dream to study science with a microscope in college. Lastly, he recorded at the bottom of the column that his dream and his family's dreams didn't line up and that he needed them to. He put words to what he was feeling and now could start working on pathways.

Under the strengths column, he listed talking to people, grammar, and knowledge of the scientific method. After a few seconds of thinking, he began to use his

FIGURE 4.2   BUILDING NEW PATHWAYS

BUILDING NEW PATHWAYS

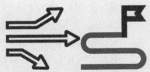

PROBLEM WHAT IS CAUSING YOU TO FEEL STUCK? WHAT MAKES THIS HARD?	STRENGTH WHAT ARE YOUR STRENGTHS? WHAT ARE YOU GOOD AT? WHAT RESOURCES COULD YOU USE?	PATHWAY HOW COULD YOU USE YOUR STRENGTH AND RESOURCES TO TACKLE THE PROBLEM?

strengths to create pathways. He took each strength and used it to build a way to work on the problem. The first pathway he created using his strength of writing was to write to a college to get more information about science careers, cultural diversity, and his potential to get into a program. His next path was to call some science labs to find out if there was more diversity in the field of microscience than what his science materials showed. Finally, he wrote that he should keep testing different ways to get to study science.

Although I knew his problem wasn't solved, he smiled as he left. He slipped me a note that said, "I'll keep you updated." Creating the pathways didn't fix the problem. However, it gave Marco hope and the confidence to keep trying to follow the path he loved.

The best part of strengthening a student's confidence in pathway planning is that it can have ripple effects on their hope score and how they tackle problems during productive struggle. For example, one of my current students told me how she used the building new pathways organizer to solve her struggles with the distributive property in algebra. I only learned how she used it because she stayed after school to show me her quiz grade. In the story, she told me how the distributive property was defeating her. She decided to try using the pathways organizer to isolate her struggling. She broke her problem down to distributing fractions and how she kept multiplying after terms were distributed.

Now that she knew the problem, it was only a matter of her remembering the errors to avoid making them. In the strengths column she listed singing, and for the first time in her life, she used her love of music to help her with math. She created a personalized song of steps and warnings as a pathway to improve and check her work.

I didn't tell her to use the tool and wasn't the one to raise her grade. She learned to use her strengths as a powerful resource. Ultimately, she was proud and wanted to show someone what she had done. I, too, was proud, but not because of her excellent grade—I was proud because she had independently formed pathways past her problem. Life doesn't come with an answer key. By teaching kids to rely on their strengths, planning, and problem-solving skills, we give them some of life's greatest gifts—the confidence to face their struggles and the self-reliance to make a path to their dreams.

HEART TO HEART

QUESTIONS AND IDEAS FOR ACTION

Reflect, discuss with a group, or share your thoughts and create a dialogue on social media using the book's hashtag, #HOPEforEdu.

Questions

1. Think of a time you were stuck on a problem. What did it feel like being stuck? How can remembering that feeling help you when you assist students who feel stuck?

2. Think of some examples of using your strengths, talents, and gifts to solve a problem. Why do you think it's essential to share problem-solving pathway examples with students?

3. Sometimes the most significant problems yield tremendous growth. What's a problem that taught you a lot about yourself? Why is it essential that our students be encouraged to try to work their way through their struggles?

Ideas for Action

- Create a school-wide picture gallery showcasing people's pathways. Have students and staff write about or illustrate a problem they faced and share the methods used to overcome it. You could include pictures to show the different ways someone worked to overcome the problem. By creating a gallery of people's pathways, we can offer encouragement and hope to students working to boost their ability to plan paths.

- Turn more complex lessons and concepts you are going to teach into games students can play. Most children are okay failing and generating new pathways during gameplay as they see it as part of "playing." Turning concepts students have difficulty with into games can help decrease anxiety about failing and allow students to work to figure out new pathways. For example, my students struggle with inference year after year, so I built an escape room in which they have to get a problem right before moving on. They work in groups to master each puzzling inference to get to the next clue. They have setbacks and they struggle, but because it's a game, they don't see the failure as much as they pay attention to the future goal of winning. During the game, to help students realize they are using pathways, consider having them write down and track the times they got behind and how they caught up or moved ahead from setbacks. Have students reflect on their pathway formation and the methods they used during the game.

BELIEF AND PLANNING PATHWAYS

We are social creatures, and with that, we set barriers for ourselves based on the images, media, and examples we surround ourselves with. Using social, cultural, and environmental cues, a person boxes themself into a belief structure and uses that structure to define their identity and future goals. Marco's family had never seen anyone like them in a science-related field, so they believed Marco did not fit the picture of a scientist.

Marco searched his school materials to prove his family wrong, but he found the lack of representation as self-fulfilling evidence of his parents' belief. His family determined what was possible based on what they knew. Using their designed belief structure, they discouraged Marco from pursuing science as they felt another path would yield better success.

What does this mean?

Representation matters.

What our students see around them positively or negatively shapes their expectations for themselves and each other. Models expand human belief and allow a person to envision a variety of futures. People need brief but meaningful contact with positive social models to gain determination and belief that their dreams are achievable. Representation allows students to create a counternarrative to what they might see or not see in the world around them. If students rarely have access to models, it can impact how they view themselves and what they accomplish.

All people make assumptions off of the models we see. Little children start forming beliefs from societal and social models early in life. Just ask any small child to draw a doctor, basketball player, teacher, mail carrier, nurse, or scientist. Their pictures can show how societal structures and prominent models have impacted them. Instead of seeing a variety of people in their drawings, you can see how the models a child has been exposed to dictate their drawings. Most likely you will notice similarities in the gender, race, or culture that students associate with certain careers. The child is not trying to perpetuate beliefs on what a person is capable of becoming, but the pictures do show how society and environmental social models shape belief structures from an early stage.

To broaden students' belief in what's possible and expand their pathways, they need to interact with successful models they identify with. They need to see various cultures, races, linguistic backgrounds, and abilities represented in the school building and in their learning. One strong model can break predefined beliefs and open the door to students envisioning themself in new roles and opportunities.

Providing students with models that increase their belief in their own achievement drives their success. The models provide evidence through their accomplishments that the path to a dream or goal is possible. Once students develop a deep belief in themselves and their potential, it acts as a self-fueling mechanism for success. In a 2021 study on college students, researchers discovered that the most robust predictor of well-being and positive outcomes was tied to the students' belief in their own achievement.[4] Simply put, having models that increase students' belief in their achievement can drive them to achieve more.

An example of modeled belief in action is evidenced in the history of the mile run. In 1945 Gunder Hagg of Sweden set the world record for the fastest mile at 4 minutes and 1.3 seconds. For years after his record, multiple athletes tried and failed to run a mile in less time. With so many failures, people started to believe humanity had found the limit of physical speed with the four-minute mile and that anything else would be physiologically impossible. Medical doctors even wrote papers about this pinnacle marker, perpetuating the belief that it was impossible to surpass the four-minute mark. This belief that four minutes was man's top speed for a mile was passed around the running world for nearly ten years.

Eventually, Roger Bannister from England conceived a belief that he could become faster by using scientific research to train. His conviction led him to try new training methods and gave him the drive to achieve his goal. Then, on a windy day in 1954, he did what was thought impossible. He ran a mile race and crossed the finish line in 3 minutes and 59.4 seconds, becoming the new world record holder for the mile.

Now here is the craziest part of this story: Within a month of Bannister's modeled time, another runner broke the four-minute mile barrier. For years people had thought it was impossible, but after Bannister broke that preconceived belief, the flood gates to achieving a mile in under four minutes opened. Bannister became a model for new possibilities. It's hard to be the first to break the mold of a belief, but once that mold is broken, it paves the way for others. Knowing Bannister's time pushed multiple athletes not to accept four minutes as the top of their game. One model helped show that more was possible.

The moment Bannister broke the time barrier, he helped the world believe there was still potential to be tapped in human speed even though society said it was impossible and doctors had recorded in medical journals that a four-minute mile was the top human speed. Today even high school athletes have achieved times of less than four minutes. However, for nearly ten years, the world would not have believed it. One model paved the way for new potential.

INCREASING REPRESENTATION WITH SOCIAL MODELS

Just as Bannister's model changed the world for runners, diverse models can change the world for our students. When students can learn about or interact with people they identify with, it gives them a chance to envision new pathways and future possibilities for their life.

Providing diverse models helps raise student belief in forging new pathways and increases academic success. A 2016 research study examining high school longitudinal data found that a school's capacity for diversity was a significant predictor of students' academic success, particularly for students from lower-income families and those who used a home language other than English.[5] Diverse models can disable stereotypes and outdated belief structures as they help provide counternarratives to negative limitations or beliefs students may have.

The first opportunity we have for students to see and interact with models is when they enter the school environment. Students must have positive diverse models reflected in what they see in schools and classrooms. Models that students identify with help them develop new goals and pathways through social modeling.

Scientific research has shown that social models build belief in what we can do through our observation of someone we consider to be like ourselves. When we see someone who we feel is like us succeed, we feel that we can succeed too. Social models increase our self-efficacy by building up our optimism in what we believe we can accomplish.[6] The more models we provide, the more kids we impact. That impact becomes a domino effect as we feed their belief, their belief leads to action, and their actions become achievement.

Wall of Achievement

Providing successful social models is a matter of responding to the populations we serve. We need to ensure students see themselves reflected in the stories they read, the bulletin boards they see, and the lessons they learn. The moment students enter school, we can increase their hope and possible pathways by providing purposeful representation.

Every child should feel they can find success in school, whether in academics, athletics, character development, or a club or activity. Showing students multiple versions of success ensures they understand there are many paths to success. It also supports students in developing new goals or pathways to try to be successful. A great way to provide social models and support student success is with a wall of achievement.

A wall of achievement serves two purposes: It celebrates student individuality and creates social models for students within the school. The wall of achievement provides a space to recognize students for school activities, clubs, academic honors, sports, competitions, and positive character development. As students gain accolades throughout the year, they get added to the wall. The wall of achievement acts as a living, breathing visual of students finding success in school.

Ideally, the wall should be located in a prominent place in the school where students can interact with it. If space is an issue, the wall could be digitized as a Google slideshow, Padlet, or Jamboard viewable through a school's web page or on monitors in the building. Students may be added to the wall in groups or individually throughout the year.

The students put on the wall should have their accomplishment honored with a picture and a space to share the story behind their achievement. If a student does not want their picture posted, an image representing the honor or accomplishment could be posted instead. Before the picture or image is posted, the student should write a sentence or two about the accomplishment and what challenges they had to overcome to achieve it.

The story shows students the pathways their social models took to reach their achievement. When we share the barriers other students have overcome, we make the achievement more attainable for others. The stories provide glimpses of the strategies and tools a student may have used to overcome obstacles on the way to success. Students can also see the effort that was involved in the achievements through the stories, which makes the models more relatable.

As students get added to the wall, consider recognizing this in school announcements throughout the year. When new additions to the wall are highlighted, students learn to focus on the positive social models in the building, thus increasing their belief in what they can accomplish. Not every kid will be a top athlete, spelling bee champ, honor roll student, valued volunteer, or award-winning artist, but by displaying the stories and faces of students that are, more kids will strive for these goals as well.

Classroom Environment: The Various Faces of Success

Improving students' belief that they can master classroom content can be enhanced by incorporating social models that reflect the students we serve. Adding social models in the classroom is a matter of purposefully surrounding students with role models relevant to the content we're teaching. Often schools will host months that celebrate people's success within a specific culture or heritage, but this is not enough.

When we introduce a concept to students, from algebraic expressions to civic leaders to figurative language, it's essential to show the faces of successful models related to that concept. Each social model we present students can help them see themselves in what they're learning. It can boost students' belief that they can learn the content and create a path to careers that utilize what they're learning.

A 2020 research study on college students shows the impact of role models in marketing materials colleges use to recruit prospective students.[7] What the researchers discovered was that prospective minority students were more willing to make similar college and major choices when presented with a role model of the same, rather than a different, ethnicity. All the school did was provide access to diverse models in their marketing materials, and this helped possible students see themselves in careers and majors they may have never considered.

If role model representation works to motivate prospective students to consider new majors or a specific college, imagine the world of possibility we open to our students by providing multiple successful role models throughout their education. The role models could disassemble barriers and increase the diversity we see in various careers.

FIGURE 4.3   WALL OF ACCOMPLISHMENT

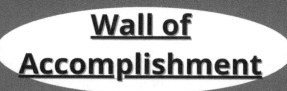

Wall of Accomplishment

Student picture

Story of how I got here

STUDENT NAME
Grade
Accomplishment

As in the study above, teachers can use pictures and stories of successful diverse people out in the world as social models for students. Using a bulletin board, producing a handout, or taking the time at the start of a unit to highlight diverse social models and telling their stories can make learning more meaningful and accessible.

Schools can also use technology to create digital spaces for students to access social models. These digital spaces can provide a place for students to connect and interact with diverse role models worldwide. There are many ways to create digital spaces for social models. One of the easiest ways is to use a site such as Flipgrid, where people can record video responses to questions. The site allows for moderation, and once videos are posted, students have access to a library of diverse models.

For example, teachers or schools could create a Flipgrid to ask questions about how different classes or units of content impact various careers. One of the first units I teach is on multiple types of writing, so I have a space for professionals to record a one-minute video on Flipgrid about how writing impacts their careers. To recruit the models, I e-mailed guardians and various business members within the community and posted a link to the grid on social media.

Each person stated their current job and talked about how writing ties into their career. There were models from the local community, some from different states, and even some from other countries. Within a day, forty to fifty videos representing a wide range of diversity were submitted to the moderated board. Some of the videos I chose to highlight to the whole class for certain parts of the unit, and that left forty responses for students to click on and see as social models in the digital space. At the start of the unit, students were given access to the Flipgrid board. They could see and hear diverse, successful professionals explaining how writing ties into their careers. It helped them see the value in writing and presented them with a wide variety of successful role models in a mix of career fields.

REPRESENTATION, BELIEF, AND DREAMS

Through increasing access to social models that are representative of the student body, we increase students' belief in what they can do and what they are capable of becoming. As students develop dreams for the future, it's important that we help them build direct pathways to begin to access their dreams. Representation with social models spurs student belief that their dream is possible. Using the dreams-to-goals graphics organizer in Figure 4.4 can help students build sustainability for their belief in reaching their dreams.

As students start to believe and dream of things they may want to be, we must keep their beliefs going past an initial spark. Representation helps students believe a way is possible. Teaching students how to feed their beliefs and start working on pathways increases their chance of reaching their dreams. The dream-to-goal pathway sheet uses two vital components to help students begin working on a path to achieve a dream.

FIGURE 4.4   DREAMS TO GOALS

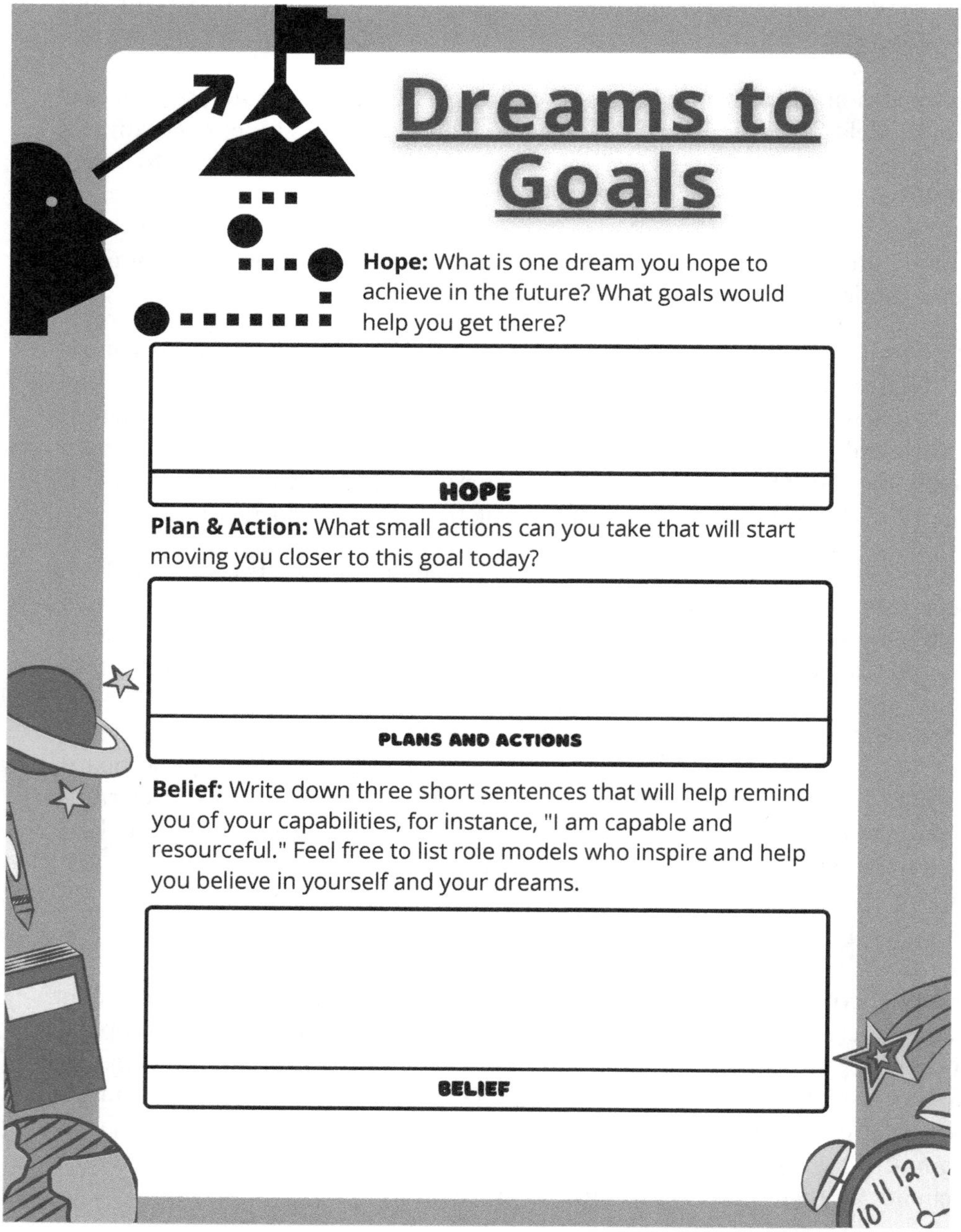

Dreams to Goals

Hope: What is one dream you hope to achieve in the future? What goals would help you get there?

> **HOPE**

Plan & Action: What small actions can you take that will start moving you closer to this goal today?

> **PLANS AND ACTIONS**

Belief: Write down three short sentences that will help remind you of your capabilities, for instance, "I am capable and resourceful." Feel free to list role models who inspire and help you believe in yourself and your dreams.

> **BELIEF**

SOURCE: Adapted from Snyder, C. (2002). Hope theory: Rainbows in the mind. *Psychological Inquiry, 13*(4), 249–275. http://jstor.org/stable/1448867

The first component on the sheet helps students think of goals that might get them to their dream. This step causes the student to form a rough initial pathway, which helps cement belief that the way is possible. Next, students think of an action they can take today to help them get to their dream. Any small action loosely tied to the dream will help build belief. When a student carries out the action, they see proof of the pathway to their dream forming, further feeding their belief. Finally, as students work towards their dream, the last section has them list self-affirmations about their capabilities and role models who inspire them that they can refer to in tough moments. By encouraging students to utilize positive affirmations and role models, this section boosts confidence, motivation, and belief during struggles.[8]

To form pathways, belief matters. What students see around them positively or negatively shapes their expectations for themselves and each other. We need to foster student belief and show them ways to kindle it when it gets low. When it comes to our classrooms and schools, we need to do our part to make sure that students can see themselves and their peers as strong, powerful, and capable of becoming anything.

HEART TO HEART

QUESTIONS AND IDEAS FOR ACTION

Reflect, discuss with a group, or share your thoughts and create a dialogue on social media using the book's hashtag, #HOPEforEdu.

Questions

1. Think of a role model who impacted your life. Who were they, and how did they impact your belief in yourself? Why were they important to you?

2. How has your background impacted your beliefs and the way you view the world? Why do you think it's necessary to see diverse social models, and how might this impact what students believe and how they view the world?

Ideas for Action

- Build and use a diversity, equity, and inclusion school checklist to ensure students can access social models representative of the student body. The checklist could include various areas of the school building and "look for's" to help staff members assess the social models provided in multiple parts of the building.

- Host career fairs either digitally or in person to allow students to see a variety of people in various roles from the community and beyond. Expose students to new career pathways that may have never been mentioned in school and to the many paths they can take after high school. Allow them to ask questions and interact with successful role models.

PROBLEMS AND PRACTICING PATHWAYS

Once students believe in and gain confidence in their ability to form pathways, they need to practice making them. To strengthen pathways, students need to face problems and learn methods to form numerous possible solutions. The exercises in this section are simple practices to help students create pathways by normalizing facing issues, showing them how to take stock of their resources, and teaching the importance of breaking down larger pathways.

Pathways are critical for success because students will face more complicated problems when they strive for more complex goals. Minor setbacks can put a big damper on any person's motivation, self-esteem, and belief in their abilities. For those with trauma and anxiety, setbacks can be detrimental if they see their problems as overshadowing their progress. When a person faces a problem, they focus on what's stopping them, and that focus can cause them to forget the progress they've made to get to that point.

Normalizing facing problems in the classroom can help a child learn how to think about an issue and discover their best tools and strategies for forming solutions. It's not that we want to normalize failure, but we want to teach that setbacks and problems can happen on the road to growth. When you encounter setbacks, it can be heart-wrenching. Your emotions may go all over the place, depending on how bad the setback is. The vital part of any setback, failure, or problem is learning from the situation. You should show students that every drawback has something to teach them that can propel them forward.

Normalizing setbacks helps alleviate the anxiety associated with failure and helps students see that losses and problems don't define them but rather *re*fine them. It doesn't mean someone is a failure or that they will not reach their goals. It's just an opportunity to practice and strengthen pathways.

The more students face problems and learn to overcome them, the more strength we add to their pathways. One of the ways I normalize facing barriers and provide students with practice to develop pathways thinking is through a simple warm-up I do every few weeks called problems to pathways.

Problems to Pathways

Problems to pathways is an activity to help students realize that they do not have to face problems alone. For many students who have had to rely on themselves during adverse childhood experiences, this idea of utilizing social support can be foreign. When a person must rely on themself for survival, it can be hard to open up and use other people as a means of support or as a resource for problems. This activity guides students to utilize social support and shows the power of collaborative problem-solving.

This warm-up takes four to five minutes. As students come into the room, they write down a problem. The problem can deal with a stuck point on a stretch goal, an academic problem they are facing, or a personal issue. The students are told not to use names or identifying information in the situation but to state the problem and why it is a sticking point.

Once students finish writing their problems, they get into two equal lines facing each other. Their partner is who they are standing across from. Should you have an odd number of students, you can join in the process. The students in one line will spend thirty seconds sharing their problems. Once the timer is up, the students in the opposite line provide ways to solve the problem for thirty seconds. Once a minute is up, the students switch, and the problem person becomes the pathway or solution giver. At the end of two minutes, students switch to a new partner and begin the process again.

Doing this for two to three rounds allows students to see that having problems is normal and that using social support can generate new pathways. This activity achieves multiple things in the classroom: It normalizes the sharing of issues, helps decrease social isolation, introduces collaborative problem-solving, and lets students practice generating pathways. This activity also sends a clear message that you care about the students' issues and their well-being. Taking just a few minutes to do this exercise allows students to feel that their problems matter in the classroom environment and see that turning to others and to education is a way to address our problems. A problem can seem impossible to overcome if the child does not have the right support and tools to form pathways.

Every student walks away from this activity with a little more hope and a little less stress. This exercise causes students to think of pathways for problems they may have never faced and grows positive class culture as everyone helps someone else. This process of collaborative support and problem-solving supports post-traumatic growth and helps with resilience following trauma.[9]

The most significant benefit from this activity is that it helps teach new ways for a student to respond to a setback. Normalizing failure detracts some of the anxiety and stress associated with setbacks and shows kids they are not alone in their failures and setbacks. This practice helps those with trauma begin to rebuild social trust in the world around them. As students work collaboratively, they experience the value social supports bring to the pathway process. The problems-to-pathways activity helps build social trust and reveals to students how collaboration can spark new ideas to turn a setback into a comeback.

Preparing for Problems

It might seem counterproductive to imagine barriers while planning pathways towards a goal, but the reality is it can help students prepare for obstacles and be ready to face them. Creating pathway milestones for larger goals increases motivation by filling a person's cup with small wins. This activity uses visualization to assist students in planning for problems and milestone markers using backward design for long-term goals.

For those with trauma and anxiety, tomorrow seems impossible when today is already overwhelming. One of my students, Wilson, didn't see a purpose in doing any future planning. His parents sent him to live with his grandma while they went to find work. His life was consumed with the move and finding out shortly after that his grandma had cancer. Teachers attempted to support him, but without any belief in his own future, he grew more apathetic. He felt stuck in the moment.

The pathway milestone tool reminds students of the power and control they have to shape their future with small wins. With Wilson and other students dealing with trauma, this process reignites hope as students see themselves progressing towards a larger future. It energizes students to care and have hope in the actions they commit daily as they can see how small actions matter to their long-term goal achievement.

When Wilson first received the pathway milestones tool at the start of the year, I told him and the other students to think of something they wanted to accomplish in the future that mattered to them. It could be a goal for this year, the next five years, or a significant life goal. It's essential to give students opportunities to share and work on their personal goals in class as it shows them you value their dreams as much as the content goals.The students work on their pathway milestones in class as a warm-up a few times in a semester, but they are free to take the tool with them to post at home, in a locker, or someplace that matters to help them keep track of the progress of their journey.

Wilson was not excited. It's important to have conversations explaining the merits of planning milestone markers, especially when you have a student who views goal setting as pointless. Wilson didn't fill anything out in class while most of the other students started planning a path to something they cared about. I sat down with him during lunch to talk about his goals and future.

"Why do I have to have goals?" Wilson asked. "People set goals, and then things happen. Life gets in the way, as it did for my grandma."

All Wilson saw was how his grandma had gotten sick, and because there was no controlling this, he found it pointless to try. I wanted him to see past the moment to realize that he shouldn't give up on having goals. I stopped talking about him and allowed him some distance by asking about his grandma.

"Does your grandma have goals?"

"Yes, she wants to finish chemo and recover."

"Is it bad that she has goals?"

Wilson sat and pondered for a moment, then he responded, "Well, no, but she doesn't decide if she recovers. You can do all the things right and fail."

"That's true. Your grandma could complete chemo and find out she still has cancer, but what if it works?"

"Well, then it's just a lucky break for her," Wilson said as he scrunched up his face.

I mirrored his body language to show him I was listening and to help him feel more comfortable. "Okay, if it's a lucky break for her, did she have any impact on the outcome?"

He responded sarcastically, "I guess *if* she recovers, she may have played a part in it."

I leaned in and said, "Well, if your grandma can play a part in her treatment, don't you want to have a say and part in who you will become?"

"I guess, but I don't know what I want to be or care about anything for school stuff. All I know is I want to help my grandma recover."

"That can be your goal."

"What? I can seriously set a goal to help my grandma recover?" Wilson's mouth hung open in disbelief.

"Does it matter to you?"

"Yes."

"Well, it sounds like the start of a good goal, but we may need to make it a bit more specific and use the pathway milestones tool to figure out the steps to help her get there. Are you okay with that?"

"Yeah. If it means I can figure out ways to help my grandma, I'll give it a go."

Wilson decided he was going to set markers that would work to support his grandma as she battled cancer. He created a plan to help her by cooking cancer-fighting foods for her. He also added that weekly he would show her survivor stories to keep up her spirit and tell her jokes because he had read articles that laughter supports physical health. This was a long path with daily steps.

He planned that she might have health setbacks along the way and that he might struggle balancing school and home life. He created plans to tell his teachers when he was struggling and ask for more time to complete assignments. If his grandma got worse, he planned to assist her by helping her focus on the positive through sharing jokes or quotes from *Green Acres*, her favorite TV show. Knowing this goal would be demanding, he took the plan with him and said he would start immediately.

I would ask Wilson about his goal progress, and he kept me updated. He went with his grandma to her major screening appointments and reported back on her health markers. In December, his grandma caught a cold that put her in the hospital. Instead of giving up, Wilson shifted his focus to the solution he had pre-planned for this. He took his original idea and modified it to giving her cards containing jokes or that showed her favorite things.

Even though December was a setback, Wilson didn't give up. He kept going, and come spring, his parents returned with steady work, and his grandma's last scan a month after her final chemo showed no signs of cancer. When Wilson brought his goal paper in, I will never forget his words, which I now use with other students: "We can't control when bad things happen, but we can push back. The small choices we make every day may feel dumb at first, but the reality is big success comes from little wins."

Letting Wilson set the goal and work on the plan in class motivated him. Not only did his goal help his grandma but it gave Wilson an anchor of control in the chaos. It showed him that his efforts were not meaningless and that what he worked at did make a difference. This activity can be a powerful tool to help a student begin mental reframing to show them that they can control their future.

The key to helping students create and utilize pathways is letting them set the goal on something that matters to them. With Wilson, his primary focus was his grandma's health, but students can select the goal using anything they're passionate about, from characteristics they want to be known for, such as being kind, to making a sports team or earning a merit badge.

The student chooses the goal and you help them figure out the key things they can do today to start on the path toward tomorrow. The backward design box has them visualize and plan from the goal backwards to the current moment, deciding on actions they can take to reach the goal. It doesn't ensure success, but as Wilson stated, it helps push the future in the direction the student is trying to go.

I do an example pathway milestones exercise with students each year. One year, I showed my students my goal to learn Brazilian jiu-jitsu. Another year I showed them a long-term goal to earn a degree. All that matters is that they see the process. Modeling your own long-term goals can help show them how to plan for their own end goal. They write down problems they think could happen on the sheet and then plan possible solutions. The critical component of this is having the student write down their *why,* or their motivation for wanting to achieve the goal. Problem-solving and sticking to long-term goals can be a struggle for all of us. However, when a person writes a clear statement of the importance of a goal, they define the worth of the goal, and, according to science, this increases their motivation.[10]

The pathway milestones exercise helps students learn to generate pathways around problems before they may be needed and lets them see how small actions add up. Investing in students' personal goals sends a clear statement that they and their dreams matter. By strengthening pathways, they learn the *how* of hope: how to plan, how to problem-solve, and how to believe in themselves. We want students to find success, and by strengthening their ability to plan pathways we ensure they'll have the tools and ability to get there.

FIGURE 4.5 PATHWAY MILESTONES

Future Goal: List in as much detail as possible what your big goal is and what it would be like to achieve it.

Backward Design: Using the end goal, what big milestones do you need to achieve to get to your goal? Starting with the milestone closest to the end goal, fill in as many big milestones as you would need to pass to reach the goal.

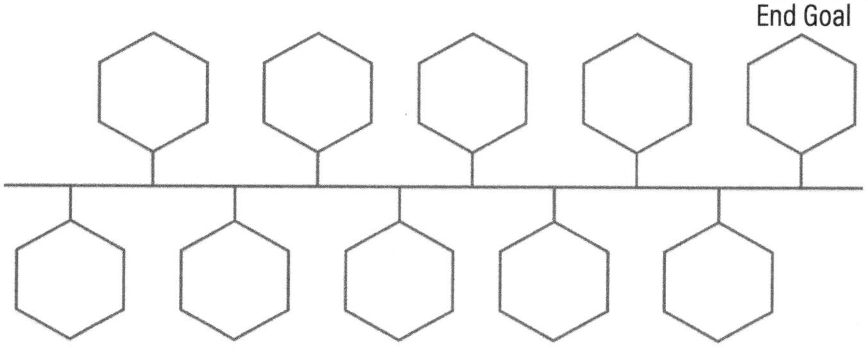

End Goal

Problems I may face on the way:	Problem-solve pathways for potential problems
■	
■	
■	
■	
■	

Motivation boost: Remember your *why*. Write a short statement on why this goal is important to you.

FIGURE 4.6 PATHWAYS DO'S AND DON'TS

Fostering Pathway Plannning to Increase 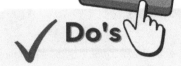 HOPE

✗ Don'ts

Don't do all the planning for your students or prevent them from experiencing productive struggle.

Don't tell students to give up or stop questioning why something isn't working.

Don't teach students to plan for obstacles without having them take stock of their strengths and resources.

Don't allow the students to be passive in learning. Using hands-on problems and experiential learning enables students to practice pathway formation.

✓ Do's

Do help students list barriers they might face on the path to a goal and help them create solutions.

Do show and help students to break longer pathways into smaller, doable steps.

Do teach students to consider failures to be the results of bad strategies or bad pathways rather than of a lack of talent.

Do provide students with social models they can use to gain belief, strategies, and tools to build pathways.

SOURCE: Adapted from Snyder, C. R. (2002). Hope theory: Rainbows in the mind. *Psychological Inquiry, 13*(4), 249–275. https://doi.org/10.1207/S15327965PLI1304_01

 **HEART TO HEART**

QUESTIONS AND IDEAS FOR ACTION

Reflect, discuss with a group, or share your thoughts and create a dialogue on social media using the book's hashtag, #HOPEforEdu.

Questions

1. There is often a stigma or fear of sharing problems with others. Think of a problem you may have dealt with on your own and a time where you shared the problem with someone else. What was the benefit of sharing the problem? What might hold someone back from sharing a problem with others? How could you use this information with students?

2. Moving on after a setback or a roadblock isn't an instant process. What are ways you refocus and keep going after a setback or problem? How could you use your example to help students during a setback?

Ideas for Action

*   When a person faces a problem or setback, they must know there are supports available to help them. Create a list of resources that can help students when they face a stuck point. You might make one list of tools for emotional support and one list of resources for academic support. This way, you guide students to care for themselves to help them bounce back and continue toward their goals.

*   Teach students to research! Often when students face a problem, they can fall into the trap of thinking they are the only one who has or has had the same problem. Having students do a simple Google search to find people who overcame a similar barrier or finding sites featuring experts on the dilemma they are facing can help them feel less isolated and help them start to generate pathways for their problem.

Compassion for Colleagues

Not having enough time, needing a restroom break, or perhaps facing an overwhelming pile of papers or tasks—most of the problems we face are calamities on a common scale. Rarely do we have to deal with dilemmas of national or world magnitude. There is an issue with the copier, planning times get taken for subbing, students are fighting—the problems we face act as little snowflakes falling on our day. They are not overwhelming…yet. However, those little snowflakes soon can fill a bucket, then a tub, and pretty soon we strain to see hope over the snowdrifts that surround us.

Two dangerous things occur in schools to prevent us from tackling our problems: problematic organizational practices and lack of support. These two components hurt our hope and, most importantly, cause educators and staff members to leave their schools. A 2020 study found that one of the most significant contributing factors to educators leaving a school was tied to organizational practices and lack of support.[1]

There are multiple hierarchies, committees, departments, and teams that separate schools into groups. Each group is in charge of certain aspects of the school or how it functions; this is meant to streamline how a school is run. The divisions should work to create a well-oiled, smoothly running school. The problem? Divisions divide. It is well known in social psychology that people define themselves by the groups they identify with.

These divisions create in-groups and out-groups in a school. Various departments, office staff, or grade levels stick together. They may intermingle at staff meetings or perhaps a social function. Groups see each other, and members might be friends with each other, but in many schools, colleagues across the various divides rarely work together on problems. A school struggling with math scores? It's the math teacher's problem to address. A giant mailing needs to be delivered tomorrow? That's the secretary's problem. Kids are struggling with trauma? That's the school counselor's problem. The reality is that all problems affect the whole school.

The divisions we create often keep us from seeing the value and strength we have together as a staff. I've heard this quoted multiple times at various professional development events: "The smartest person in the room is the room." If we relegate a problem to only one source to solve, if a person sitting in an office or a different group has a strength that could help with that problem, they can't offer solutions.

I've seen amazing colleagues rise to meet problems and deadlines all by themselves but at the cost of overwhelming stress and their mental health. You might be that person who does it all for the school, being praised for a moment for doing so much. Then, when the glow of the praise fades, you begin the cycle again of doing too much, mistaking the relief from all the pressure and pain as enjoyment in helping.

Often our independence can act as a sword that cuts down our support. It's great to have independent colleagues. However, it's equally imperative that they never get to the point where they are too independent to call someone else for help. You see, a school is like a band. Yes, the flute is wispy and happy and can play on its own, and so can the sax with its smooth and mellow tones. The drum is reverberating and powerful as it plays a solitary tune. They can all work independently, but when they become unified in a song, they gain power. Together they make magic.

Each person who comes into a school has strengths, life experience, resources, and tools they bring to the table. The more methods and moments we create for the band of colleagues to come together and work on issues, the more harmony we create for the individual members.

Staff Strengths Directory

One practice that can help us see and utilize the strengths of our fellow staff members is a staff strengths directory. In this practice, each staff member lists their talents, skills, certifications, and areas of professional expertise. It's crucial for staff members to be specific when listing their abilities because their skills will become resources other colleagues may call upon to address problems or meet goals.

For example, one teacher may struggle with classroom engagement. Instead of going it alone, he uses the directory and notices a colleague who lists engagement with gamification as a strength. Typically the two wouldn't talk, since one teaches math and the other art, but the directory provides a pathway to bring staff together to utilize the strengths that lie inside the school.

A lot of staff members do their jobs behind closed doors. The staff strengths directory helps display the jewels that are hidden in a building. The greatest resource for each of us lies in the strengths of the people right down the hall.

Problem Inventory

Sometimes when a person thinks about a problem for a long time, they can become fixated on the situation and miss solutions. Research has shown that functional fixedness prevents people from fully seeing all the options that might be available to find a solution.[2] Functional fixedness can cause us and our colleagues to feel stuck and unsupported. One of the ways schools can prevent functional fixedness is through creating a pathway to share problems to kick-start solutions.

School leadership teams can create a system to share problems and solutions through a problem inventory. A problem inventory is a place for staff members to list issues that are making them feel stuck. To get more staff members to feel comfortable sharing problems, they should be able to choose to give their problem anonymously or publicly. By providing the choice to remain anonymous, we allow our colleagues to avoid feelings of being shamed or shunned for not finding solutions. Problems could be collected digitally through a Google Form or through a box that sits in a central location staff could access.

The key aspect of collecting the problems is to make sure staff include as many details as possible to clearly describe the issue they are facing. Staff should eliminate identifying information if they want to submit their problem anonymously. Once all the problems for a month are collected, leadership teams in a school should meet to come up with one to three possible solution pathways for each situation.

After the possible solutions are created, they should be shared with the individuals who identified themselves. For individuals who chose to remain anonymous, their solutions could be made available as a handout at a staff meeting. Leadership teams could also display the problems at staff meetings and give a time frame in which staff members could work together to develop a variety of solutions for various colleagues' concerns.

By creating a system to share problems, we can offer solutions and support when others feel stuck and vulnerable. This organizational practice works to counteract the isolation and lack of support that can cause colleagues to leave. A problem inventory allows us to share our burdens when we feel helpless, giving each of us strength, support and, most importantly, hope.

Preventing Problems

Sometimes the best way to solve a problem is to prevent it from forming in the first place. Proactive solutions work by analyzing trends in the current problems generated in a school to build systems and practices to stop those problems from arising. When leadership teams or staff develop solutions for problems, they also need to look at the inventories to analyze for systematic issues.

Our vantage point and perceptions can cause us to miss that minor problems may have stemmed from more extensive problems. For instance, staff might list issues like:

- *Sometimes I need to use the restroom but can't go because I would leave my students alone.*

- *I want to observe a teacher, but she has to plan when I do.*

- *I need to schedule a meeting with a parent, but it's during a class.*

Those minor problems could be solved as they come up, but they indicate a more significant problem: Staff need built-in flex time that they can access. This bigger problem could be taken care of by creating a system for emergency flex time in which someone can cover a class or take on someone's responsibility for a few minutes, or planned flex time when someone knows they need coverage. If we don't take the time to figure out their root causes, the same minor problems will keep arising. In this case, colleagues will keep presenting problems indicating the need for flexible time with coverage. By identifying underlying problems, schools can isolate systematic issues that burden staff members.

A simple way to discover trends in problems is to take the time to group them into specific categories. Researchers Zavelevsky and Lishchinsky created an ecological model of school culture that groups problems into categories known to impact culture (p. 112).

By categorizing problems into these various groups, it helps us begin to see commonalities that might stem from more significant issues. Once a more prominent issue has been identified, it is only a matter of implementing a proactive solution and monitoring new problems that come in to see if the more significant problem has been fixed or needs further action.

Enhancing Well-Being to Prevent Problems

In addition to preventing staff problems from forming, it's vital to be proactive about staff well-being. It's a well-known fact that a person's physical and mental health can impact how well they think and work. There are a variety of practices that can work to increase employee wellness in a school. As schools work to proactively support employee wellness, they are also simultaneously providing protection against staff developing specific physical, social, and mental problems. Creating a well-rounded employee wellness program for school staff also increases staff morale and can foster a sense of togetherness.

Collaboration Spaces

To foster collaboration and communication between colleagues and promote employee wellness, consider setting up collaboration spaces for staff. The room should be comfortable and contain items that will help foster staff wellness. For example, it might include whiteboards for staff members to share personal goals or work on ideas. This type of space can also be used to post staff wellness challenges, funny jokes, or inspirational quotes as a pick-me-up for staff. The purpose of the area is to create a retreat that staff members can use to revitalize themselves during the school day.

Promoting Gratitude

Research studies show that gratitude is positively correlated with happiness, hope, and overall better mental well-being.[3,4] Making gratitude a foundational component in a school can increase the happiness and outlook of all staff. Ultimately, the more a person practices gratitude, the more they train their brain to look for and focus on the positive in the world around them. This mental shift allows a person to experience negative moments but still notice the good in their circumstances. Practicing gratitude over time also

FIGURE 4.7   THE ECOLOGICAL SCHOOL CULTURE

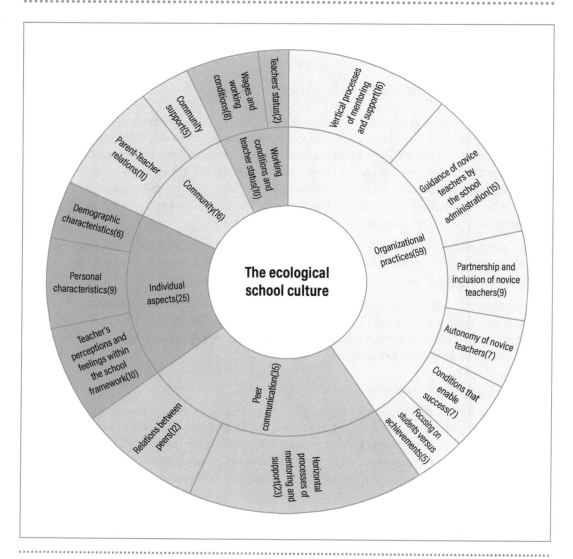

SOURCE: Zavelevsky, E., & Lishchinsky, O. S. (2020). An ecological perspective of teacher retention: An emergent model. Teaching and Teacher Education, 88, 102965. https://doi.org/10.1016/j.tate.2019.102965

impacts the social bonds inside an organization. As our colleagues get more appreciation from others at work, they gain greater job satisfaction, improve relationships with other staff members, and experience greater motivation. Gratitude creates a work culture of support that research has shown results in less stress and burnout.[5]

To promote more gratitude in a school, consider creating challenges with rewards to get staff members in the habit of practicing gratitude. Schools could set a goal for colleagues to write short notes of appreciation and track the progress by e-mail. Staff members could blind copy a person in charge of keeping track of the letters, and rewards could be given for meeting a specific target or being at the top.

Incentivizing gratitude will allow you and your colleagues to develop it as a habit. Once it's a habit, it will improve the culture and well-being of every member of the school. The best part of this challenge is that even staff who do not participate will want to join after receiving a small grateful note from a colleague. With gratitude as a defining value, schools become well-equipped to provide the kind of supportive, uplifting work environment all staff members need to thrive.

Staff Newsletters and Wellness Wednesdays

A lot of schools have staff newsletters that include upcoming events and important dates to remember. Staff newsletters could also be used to provide quick tools employees could use to improve their overall wellness. Putting out a staff newsletter containing crucial information and wellness tips shows that employee well-being is just as important as the school's functioning.

There are multiple websites that provide wellness tips daily, monthly, or weekly. By subscribing to one and linking the information to the staff newsletter, a simple couple of clicks can provide resources for staff members to improve their self-care tools. The wellness section could even go so far as to offer quick tips for mind, body, and overall happiness. The goal of the wellness section is to provide your colleagues the gift of new tools to try to improve their lives. By highlighting different strategies and tools that improve a person's wellness, we pass on more resources employees can use to take care of themselves.

Instead of just putting tips on paper, we can challenge our colleagues to practice new wellness tips and strategies once a week by implementing Wellness Wednesdays. On an announcement or in a school broadcast, a person could highlight one wellness tip from the staff newsletter or a specific website and challenge the school to implement that tip on Wellness Wednesday. The practice of Wellness Wednesday is beneficial for multiple reasons. First, it gives all staff members a chance to practice the wellness tip of the day, and it models to students that self-care is essential and prioritized in the school building. Plus, Wednesday is midway through the week—a time when many school employees and students might need an extra boost to get to the end of the week. By offering wellness challenges such as performing a random act of kindness, trying deep breathing, using mindfulness tools, or telling jokes, we give staff and students a chance to learn new ways to keep themselves feeling at their best.

When we make staff feel supported with tools and resources, we enhance their ability to plan pathways around obstacles. It's essential to be cautious about overplanning for staff members, however. Giving proactive support and resources assists employees in forming their own pathways. Assisting fellow employees in making their own paths rather than giving them answers shows them that their input and thoughts matter. These practices help strengthen employees' confidence in their ability to plan pathways and figure out a way to a goal. As our colleagues gain self-confidence that their input and thoughts matter in a school, they become more invested in the school and more energized to tackle problems as they arise.

Education can be an isolating profession, but we can break barriers that box us in by providing pathways and proactive solutions to problems. The reality is that we're not alone, and by shifting organizational practices and support, we can support each other when facing problems. It is the support and resources we provide that determine if we mope, cope, or gain hope!

CHAPTER 5

ENERGIZING

Mary was witty, she could problem-solve past barriers or argue a point grace-fully, and her goals were fantastic, but she was burnt out.

One day a message appeared in my e-mail. It was cc'd to Mary's teachers. It sim-ply stated she would not be in class and to send her work to in-school detention. I went down to see her.

Through the window on the door, I saw Mary sitting in a cubicle, staring at a computer. Her hood was up, and with Mary, that meant her defenses were up, too. Shadows danced on the white walls as the fluorescent lights flickered over-head. Besides the monitoring teacher, Mary was alone. Hearing me enter the small space, she turned, rubbed her eyes, and looked at me wearily. As I walked over to her, she pulled the strings of her hood tighter as if burying herself in her hoodie, creating a tomb of grey fabric.

What do you do when disappointment sets in? When temptations scream your name and your goals and dreams only whisper? When hurt steals your hope, and you want to give up?

Mary was there. A loss of willpower can happen slowly over a long period or sud-denly due to a recent event or situation. When willpower hits an all-time low, we can develop a feeling known as burnout. Mary's story may seem familiar because in the past few months, you may have felt this way as well. Burdens from a global pandemic. Family problems. Technology that constantly beeps and buzzes, demanding your attention. Blurred lines between work and home. Feeling pulled from all sides.

I pulled a chair up to Mary. After a few moments of silence, she pulled back her hood slightly so her face appeared as a circle hugged in grey fabric. The opening of the hood signaled to me that she was now ready to talk. I looked inquisitively at her as I sat silently. Seeming to know the question I wanted to ask, Mary took a deep breath. In a low, shaky voice, she began to speak.

"I messed up. Before you say anything, I didn't hurt anyone. I was caught with a vape."

I moved closer to the cubicle where she sat and said, "Everyone messes up. What's important is that you learned something to put in your toolbox."

She scrunched her face into a sneer. It was a wonder she could squeeze words past her tight lips. "Yeah, right. I have tools, but they don't work. I'm tired of fighting to do normal things. I try and get nowhere." Her words were angry, and as she spoke them, she drew back into the protection of her hood.

The teacher monitoring the small room nodded as if in agreement.

We sat. Time crept by at a snail's pace. The clock's second hand ticked like a metronome. Despite what I wanted to say or how I wanted to lead the conversation, I waited. It was crucial Mary control the conversation, especially when her life might be feeling out of control.

Silence.

After a few minutes of patiently waiting, Mary's head emerged again from her fabric shell. Her eyes traced the lines on the ceiling as she took another long, slow breath and said, "Look, my dad started drinking again. I told him to stop. I told him not to, but he doesn't listen. With all my family junk, it's hard to focus. Doing good in school is my way out. I want it more than anything. But I have three tests that I'm not ready for and a mountain of homework. I don't feel good. I want good grades, but it's impossible! Why try if I'm going to fail? I'm tired."

She rested her head on her clenched hand. Minus the hoodie, she looked like that statue of The Thinker as she gazed at the wall and asked, "Have you ever felt you were fighting a losing battle?"

I nodded. "Yes. I think every person has felt that way at one time. You know what helps? Big battles are easier with an army at your side. Why didn't you tell someone?"

Mary sat back and crossed her arms defensively. "Because I didn't want to. I tried to take care of things. Today was too much. This morning one of my brother's friends offered me a vape, and I took it. I went to the bathroom. I wanted to feel better. I got caught. So here I am." She sunk her hands deep into the pockets of her hoodie.

"I'm done pretending things are fine. They aren't. I can't get the grades I want. I can't do anything. I might as well just enjoy the moment cuz my willpower's gone." She slumped over and the fabric of her hood covered her whole head like grey clouds invading on a sunny day.

I waited a moment until her breathing started to settle to a more even rhythm and then said, "Mary, your willpower isn't gone." I paused, realizing she needed to know she wasn't alone. "We can get through this together. You don't have to fight alone."

The hood came down completely as she tilted her head up to ask, "Okay, then what's the plan?"

Mary thought she could tackle her problems at first. Her motivation and willpower shifted when her perception changed. At first, she felt her problems were small hills to be attacked, but as more problems arose and time dragged on, her hills became a Mt. Everest of issues. To her, the way seemed impossible. In her moment of struggle, she gave up.

Although Mary felt her willpower disappear, the reality is willpower doesn't rely on an internal energy source. As Dr. Michael Inzlicht, a scientific researcher on self-control and motivation at the University of Toronto, explains, "This notion that self-control relies on a resource that has depleted, such as a mental fuel that runs out after use, I think that's deeply wrong."

As Inzlicht points out,

> Ego depletion [or this loss of willpower] is more like a form of fatigue. We get tired, and everyone knows that we have different capacities at the end of the day because we have different interests and motives than at the beginning of the day.

> So fatigue is real. Fatigue impacts cognition. That's also real. For example, I've got some research showing that you might show some measurable deficits in memory and learning after about an hour. So after an hour of learning, you may notice students drifting off and find they have less of a capacity to learn. I think we do get tired. And when we are tired, our abilities, including our ability to restrain ourselves [or use willpower], becomes diminished.

Dr. Inzlicht's research explains what happened to cause Mary to end up burnt out using a dual process model. In this model, self-control or willpower comprises two key elements: motivation and attention for a given task. Our motivation and attention interact with each other like cogs to create self-control. As shifts with both happen, they impact each other and can lead to burnout. So, willpower depletion or burnout is not a mysterious draining of a mental resource but occurs from shifts in emotion, attention, and motivation.

Mary was unaware that her lack of hopeful agency played a big part in her lack of will. When Mary took the Children's Hope Scale at the start of the school year, she scored low in the agency section. Students with low agency scores have little confidence in their ability to achieve their goals. In other words, Mary has low self-efficacy. She has lots of great ideas with a high pathway score, but she ends up going nowhere due to low self-efficacy.

As Dr. Inzlicht explains,

> You need to feel you are effective in the world—that you have self-efficacy—to even bother trying. A person who feels they shouldn't even

FIGURE 5.1   DUAL-PROCESS MODEL OF SELF-CONTROL

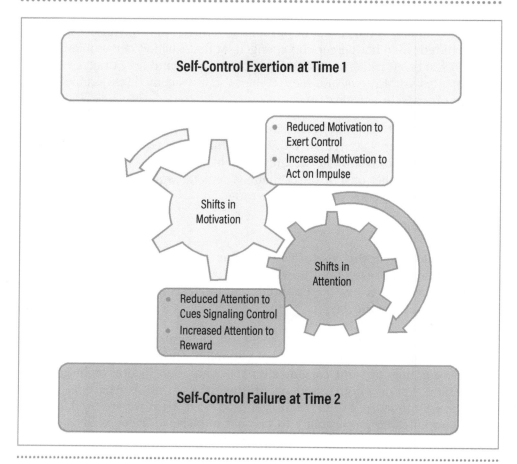

SOURCE: Inzlicht, M., & Schmeichel, B. J. (2012). What is ego depletion? Toward a mechanistic revision of the resource model of self-control. *Perspectives on Psychological Science, 7*(5), 450–463. https://doi .org/10.1177/1745691612454134

bother trying will fall prey to just doing what's good for them right now. This is the opposite of willpower, where a person says no to things for right now and, by doing that, says yes to something in the future. For example, a person may study now not because studying is fun but because if they continue studying for twelve years, they'll hopefully have a better life than they could have otherwise.

[Ultimately] when you believe that your actions have outcomes in the world, you are more willing to engage in effort. We have brain correlates of that engagement. Whereas if your actions are disconnected from what you experience, then you disengage.

A person's appraisals [or beliefs] influence the extent to which they are willing to engage in effort. So I think a big part of willpower is, are you willing to work? It's a motivational question, and appraisals drive motives. If you think something's impossible, then you're not going to do it. Why would you? That doesn't make any sense. So hope may play a role with the appraisals a person forms.

HOPE AND WILLPOWER

Psychologist Dr. Rick Snyder showed the world how hope and willpower are connected when he appeared on a two-hour special on *Good Morning America (GMA)* in 2000. Dr. Snyder conducted a live experiment on national television using the host, the medical expert, and the weather guy. All three cast members agreed to participate in the cold pressor task. The task required each person to dunk their hand into freezing water and hold it there for as long as possible. All three members quickly put their hands in, but after a few minutes, the weatherman pulled his hand out, shaking it to warm it up. Only two cast members then remained in the frigid water: the host and the medical expert.

The two men went eye to eye in a battle of will. As the episode came close to ending, the medical expert pulled out his hand, shaking his head in disbelief at the host. The host then did something surprising: He turned to the camera and vowed to remain in the water until the end of the commercial. After a few agonizing minutes, the commercial break ended, and the show's host removed his hand, victorious but confused. He questioned Dr. Snyder as to what hope had to do with cold water and his winning.

Dr. Snyder revealed to the audience that before the show, he had given all three cast members the Adult Hope Scale. He pulled out their scores then proceeded to show the audience that their scores accurately predicted who would come in first, second, and third. The host's high hope was tied directly to his will to withstand the pain of the task and reach the goal of winning the challenge. Snyder showed the world at that moment how hope fuels our willpower to keep going even amid struggle.

Just as high hope was used to predict the outcome of the cold pressor task, it also, according to research, predicts students' academic attainment, engagement, and grade point average,[1,2] which all take a level of self-control or willpower, and hope helps willpower. Students with hopeful perceptions (which can be brought about via intervention) are more likely to engage in success-oriented academic behaviors, which has been shown in various studies to result in higher academic success and higher hope.[3,4] That's why it's critical we foster and develop hope, and with students who have low hope in agency, this starts by assisting them with willpower.

Willpower is impacted by our perceptions of the world and ourselves. Trauma can alter a person's perception of their power and effectiveness, and tough times can trigger poor decisions. Moments of struggle can make us seek relief. Momentary relief is good, but when we stop believing in our effectiveness and temptations override our drive to pursue goals and dreams, we lose our future.

The key to helping students overcome a moment of struggle is not to down-play the struggle's difficulty but to offer strategies to persevere. Self-control helped the host on *GMA* win the challenge, but it didn't save him from the struggle. The strategies he used gave him the power to keep going as the temptation to quit beckoned through the pain.

TOOLS FOR PREVENTING WILLPOWER FAILURE

One way to assist students to achieve their goals, build agency, and prevent burnout is to teach strategies to combat temptation. Temptation is a part of life; it promises gratification in the form of distraction, entertainment, and socialization. The world around us is filled with advertising and cues for food, goods, products, and instantaneous gratification. Even tools that promise to help us be more productive, such as computers and cellphones, can tempt and distract us with social media, games, and streaming services. The environments we interact with frequently cue desires that conflict with our goals.

The key to fighting temptation is not exerting monumental self-control but learning strategies to make self-control more effective in any given moment. Dr. Inzlicht explains, "The research by Angela Duckworth and James Gross (2016) focuses on a process model for self-control. They break down self-control into various points of entry. The major contribution their research suggests is that willpower acts like an emergency brake. It's like a just-in-time tool to pay attention right now to what you're doing."

Dr. Inzlicht elaborates,

> For example, imagine your phone goes off in class. You might push away the phone; you might will yourself not to look at it, but you've already lost the battle once the phone is out. If you have to rely on willpower, you're likely to fail. In fact, we've got research showing that if you're tempted by something, that's a major contributor to goal failure. Whether you use self-control or not doesn't matter. Yes, you might have some successes here and there, but globally, if you're tempted by the thing, you're done, you're finished. So you have to avoid being tempted to begin with, and that's where you can think of various strategies that you can mount to combat temptation."

So, preventing temptation is important rather than relying solely on willpower once the temptation has occurred.

The process model of self-control showcases various strategies that help boost goal success and agency. There are four main strategies that can assist with self-control: situational strategies, attentional strategies, appraisal strategies, and, as a last resort, response strategies. Using more strategies increases the likelihood students will reach their goals and avoid willpower failure or burnout.

FIGURE 5.2 PROCESS MODEL OF SELF-CONTROL

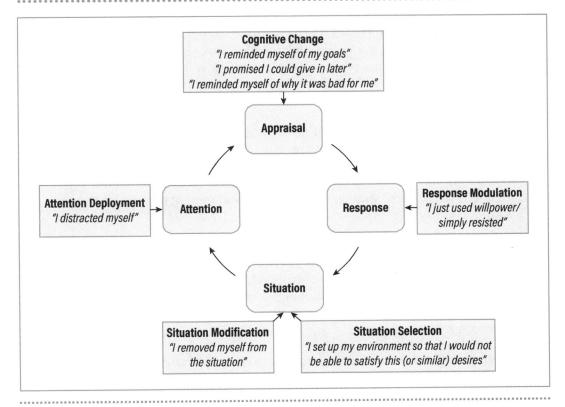

SOURCE: Duckworth, A. L., Gendler, T. S., & Gross, J. J. (2016). Situational strategies for self-control. *Perspectives on Psychological Science, 11*(1), 35–55. https://doi.org/10.1177/1745691615623247

Situational Strategies

The first strategy that we can teach to assist willpower and prevent burnout is situation modification. Students can use forward thinking to create plans to avoid temptation and meet goals. One way to modify a situation is through precommitment. Precommitment works on the same principle as the self-care plan in Chapter 2. Self-care plans help students prepare in advance how to handle a moment of mental stress by analyzing and planning to use their coping mechanisms. Precommitment works similarly, except the plan provides students with strategies to avoid or reduce temptations in specific situations or to choose situational circumstances that suit their goals. The key is thinking ahead.

Precommitment happens when a person intentionally acts to limit their future options in order to enforce commitment to a specific goal. Dr. Inzlicht explains, "I am a big fan of precommitment. I have issues with the Internet. At one point, I could not stop checking Twitter, and it became problematic for me. I now have an app that shuts down various websites that I choose, and now I could not get on Twitter even if I wanted." Inzlicht's example shows how planning for a future situation by modifying the temptations you have access to can help students gain success.

Everyone faces temptations. Perhaps you've used this strategy, like Dr. Inzlicht? Maybe by choosing not to buy junk food because you know you'll eat it? Maybe by putting money in a place you can't touch so you know you'll save it? Maybe by turning off the Wi-Fi at dinner so you know you can have quality time with the family?

People with high self-control use strategies such as precommitment to help with temptations. Strategies are typically learned through trial and error over a lifetime. With the temptations in the world mounting, it's imperative students have tools for the difficulties they'll face. They should actively be taught self-control strategies such as precommitment to improve their will and their success.

As a matter of fact, Dr. Inzlicht's suggestion of precommitment is a strategy many students with high self-control already know and utilize. A 2015 study found that students with more self-control and higher academic standing report having fewer distractions when studying, showing precommitment to the task.[5] One way to teach precommitment is to offer students the ability to fill out and use a precommitment contract.

The precommitment contract can be used for a goal such as needing to study or work. Having students think about the environment where they typically study gives them a chance to consider possible temptations. On the form, they write down the temptations that they think might appear when they study. This gives students a chance to utilize the contract to learn how precommitment works to reduce or eliminate temptations.

Students can then use one of the checkboxes on the precommitment contract, such as removing the temptation from the environment (for example, by moving a video game system or working in an environment without a television). Students should also be encouraged to think of other ways to limit temptations, such as having a parent or guardian check in on them while studying to check their progress. Through the precommitment contract, they can begin to internalize how the strategy works so they can use it any time, even without the contract.

Once students decide on a future action to avoid their temptations, they should think of a way to reward themself if they follow through. Multiple research studies show that offering yourself an extrinsic reward for achieving a task or goal helps increase the intrinsic motivation and positive feelings associated with the given task.[6,7] The key is to make sure the reward is something the student enjoys, like taking a nature walk, calling a friend, drawing a picture, reading some jokes, playing a game, or listening to their favorite song. After deciding on the reward and what they will do to earn the reward, have the student write a date or cue they should use to enact their plan. It's vital to provide time frames and cues to help students act on their precommitment contracts.

FIGURE 5.3   PRECOMMITMENT CONTRACT

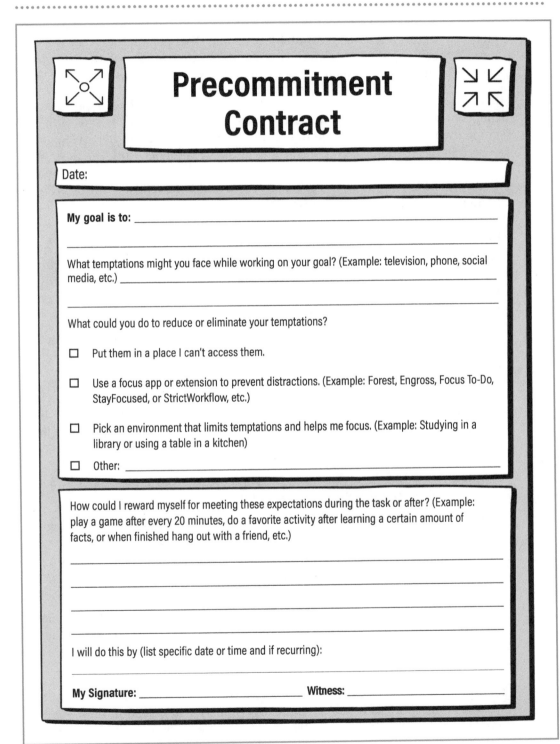

Precommitment Contract

Date: _____

My goal is to: _____
_____

What temptations might you face while working on your goal? (Example: television, phone, social media, etc.) _____
_____

What could you do to reduce or eliminate your temptations?

☐   Put them in a place I can't access them.

☐   Use a focus app or extension to prevent distractions. (Example: Forest, Engross, Focus To-Do, StayFocused, or StrictWorkflow, etc.)

☐   Pick an environment that limits temptations and helps me focus. (Example: Studying in a library or using a table in a kitchen)

☐   Other: _____

How could I reward myself for meeting these expectations during the task or after? (Example: play a game after every 20 minutes, do a favorite activity after learning a certain amount of facts, or when finished hang out with a friend, etc.)

_____
_____
_____
_____

I will do this by (list specific date or time and if recurring):
_____

My Signature: _____   **Witness:** _____

The last precommitment strategy used in the contract is announcing intentions in order to increase follow-through. Announcing intentions boosts commitment because it adds in an element of social accountability. Students can use a peer, guardian, or teacher as an accountability person. That person then acts as a witness to the student's precommitment. The signature will remind the student of the public affirmation, which will help them follow through on their plan.

It's critical to create a way for students to access copies of their precommitment contracts throughout the year as various self-control needs arise. This will guide them through precommitment until it becomes part of their self-control repertoire. Precommitment contracts could help students work on class projects, study for assessments, or plan for independent work in the classroom. Getting students to make and practice precommitment as a strategy benefits all students, especially those who struggle. According to research, it can help the most impulsive people (those with the weakest willpower) be more effective at meeting their goals.[8]

The precommitment contract was a game-changer for Mary. Her father's drinking and the overwhelming academic tasks made her feel like trying was pointless. Mary relied on willpower to force herself through difficult moments. Her go-to strategy worked some days, but on others it led her to feel completely burnt out.

"I push. Even with all the crap, I study. It's so tiring. I just want relief sometimes. I sat down to study and with all I had to do, just lost it," Mary said as she shrugged her shoulders.

I opened my palms and spoke softly. "Mary, your willpower is admirable, but you're going to get tired. When we're tired, it's harder to use willpower to fight temptations. You don't want to wait until the heat of the moment to decide how to handle difficult situations. That would be like trying to come up with an escape plan in the middle of a battle. The best time to handle temptations and acts of will is before they happen. Do you think we can create a precommitment contract so you don't feel so burnt out again?" I held out the paper.

Mary nodded and grabbed the paper. She tapped her finger while thinking out loud. "I want to write that my goal is to get my dad to stop drinking, but I can't control that. I have control over what I become, so I need to do okay today despite all the world drama and my dad's drinking. It's just impossible to do in my house. I fight myself to do stuff by force, and it drains all my energy."

I asked Mary, "Well, how could you change the situation? Could you change where you work, or when you work? How could you make the situation easier so you could use your energy for other battles?"

For a few minutes, Mary thought about her situation. Then she said, "I do better when I study over at my neighbor's house. Last week I went over there to work and her mom said I could come any time. Her room has a lot of sunlight and lamps, and there's a small table with chairs. Because her room is on the top floor, it's really quiet. Plus, she has like a bazillion plants that make it seem like a peaceful jungle.

"Since we had similar classes, we worked together to finish homework, and it felt easy. I had a better week then and didn't feel so burnt out. It kept me from being around all the family stuff while trying to work. I could ask her mom if I could come over there to keep away from everything. Do you think you could check in on me and ask me how it goes?"

I pointed to the bottom of the contract and said, " I would be happy to ask you about how the precommitment works out, but what about a reward for yourself?"

She rubbed her forehead as she thought. "I could just talk to my friend for a bit and maybe look at some funny memes. That would make me feel happy, just like a reward. I filled out the whole contract. Will you sign my contract with me?"

"Sure," I replied.

Every work week I would follow up and ask Mary how her precommitment to study was going. She often told me things were "just fine," and after a couple of weeks of questioning, she stopped me in the hallway.

"You know the hard things are still hard. My father is still drinking. My house is still crazy most days. But because of making this one thing easier, I have more fight left in me. Before, I pushed myself through so many things. I hated school-work. By studying with my neighbor every night, it's become like an autopilot thing. Plus, my grades don't suck now, and it's kind of epic that I did it." She smiled as she walked away.

ATTENTIONAL STRATEGIES

Sometimes we end up in situations where temptations are unavoidable. For example, a student may have a love for computer games. Their precommitment strategy for studying might be to put away the computer while working. But what if a teacher requires every child to use a computer for an assignment? Then the temptation is only a click away. The student doesn't want to use the computer, but the computer must be used. The precommitment strategy doesn't work. When temptations are unavoidable, attentional strategies can assist with willpower.

Attentional strategies work by drawing a person's focus away from temptations while working on a task. One of the easiest attentional strategies to teach students to use right away is self-monitoring. Self-monitoring works to focus a person's attention on what they're doing when around temptations. Students can learn to keep track of their focus and behavior through notes, a journal, or a spreadsheet when they feel temptations can't be avoided. They record their actions without judgment and use that to help improve focus.

For example, the boy with the video game temptation could write on a piece of paper what he is doing every ten minutes to divert his attention from the temptation of playing a computer game. He might click on the game and then to self-monitor record on the paper that he got distracted. Taking the time to record his actions keeps him in the moment and allows him to reevaluate his decision without judgment. Self-monitoring works because performing a concurrent task when tempted diminishes the power of temptations around you and can promote self-control.[9]

A step above self-monitoring is assisting students in developing mindfulness to use as an intentional attentional strategy. The grounding techniques discussed in the first chapter work along the same lines as mindfulness. Grounding techniques help a person to shift focus to stay "in the moment" when their mind and body have a trauma or stress response. The difference is that mindfulness goes a step further to get a person to calmly acknowledge and accept their feelings, thoughts, and bodily sensations in a nonjudgmental way. Numerous free guided mindfulness exercises on YouTube could be done with students and require little to no prep work or training. They are typically quick exercises that take one to five minutes.

Mindfulness is a skill that takes time to develop. Implementing a Mindfulness Monday or daily mindfulness routine encourages students to practice mindfulness during the day. Building mindfulness into the daily or weekly schedule allows students to practice and hone their skills and over time leads to numerous benefits, such as helping with self-control or willpower, alleviating stress and anxiety, and increasing creativity.[10]

Neuroimaging has shown that diverting attention from temptation can help decrease intrusive thoughts and lead to more engagement in the prefrontal brain regions associated with learning and thinking.[11] Ultimately, these attention strategies shift focus, supporting a person to keep going past distractions and temptations.

APPRAISAL STRATEGIES

Another strategy students can use is to change the way they think. Appraisal works through reframing a situation or thought. Through reappraisal, a person can change the value or worth of a temptation or change the way they think about their abilities or potential in a given moment.

One of the quickest and easiest appraisal strategies is reappraising a temptation in a negative light. Dr. Inzlicht explains: "Let's say you have a piece of candy. Reappraisal allows you to think about the thing differently. Like maybe that food that you're so tempted by, you can reappraise it by imagining it has been sitting on a store shelf for ten days, and it's moldy." By taking the time to imagine the temptations in front of us in a different light, we can convince our minds that they will be less gratifying and increase our self-control by shifting our perception of the temptation. To teach students to shift appraisals, use guided imagination activities to show them how to reappraise a temptation. The tactic of having students think of their favorite foods and then what would make those foods unappealing can help them understand how to utilize reappraisal for temptation.

Reappraisal can also be used to increase student motivation and focus on a given task. For instance, a student facing a complex math problem could reframe the work as putting them one step closer to their dream of computer programming instead of thinking of it as just another problem. Teachers can foster reappraisal for assignments by keeping students' long-term goal papers in a place where they are accessible to the student. Having their goals nearby allows the student to use those goals to reappraise moments in the present using motivation for the future.

My oldest son used appraisal strategies to get through his last year of high school during the pandemic. Virtual and hybrid learning disrupted his senior year and decreased his motivation. Midterms came, and he was doing poorly in three of his four classes. The pandemic made life seem out of control and flooded him with memories of early abuse from his biological parents. He complained, "This is my senior year, and it's not fair! I already had my birth parents ruling over me, hurting me, and trying to kill me, and now I have a pandemic trying to kill me, taking away my senior year and my friends, and dictating what I can do."

He went on. "You know why my grades suck? Because I just don't care. Because it could all be taken away in an instant. School could shut down again. COVID canceled homecoming and will probably cancel my graduation like it did for the seniors last year. What is the point? We are all at the mercy of an invisible killer. Now instead of my dad isolating me for abuse, COVID is."

I told him, "All of these changes are hard, and I hear you say it isn't fair, and you're right. It isn't. Bad things have happened. The pandemic has changed a lot, but the pandemic does not control you or what you become. You do.

"Yes, the pandemic has changed your senior year from what you were expecting. It has taken things away, but don't let it steal your future. You want to join the military and you can still do that. You can still become a teacher. You can still change the world. It might be more difficult. That's why you should remind yourself why all the work is worth it. Why spending hours in a virtual class is worth it. Why your senior year isn't about the graduation or homecoming but about you getting one step closer to reaching your dreams."

He took a deep breath and just sat for a minute with his head cupped in his hands.

"You're right. I'll bring my grades up. I'm going to call the army recruiter tomorrow."

Within a week, his room was filled with army merchandise. He spent his weeks purposefully connecting to his recruiter. He surrounded himself with reminders of his goal. By the end of the nine weeks, he had raised his grade and passed the physical test for the army. I spoke to him about his grades one night before he left to meet his recruiter.

"You should be proud of yourself for bringing up your grades. What did you do differently?"

"After I broke down, I realized my problem was that I saw school as part of the pandemic. After we talked, I started thinking about school as a stepping stone, not something to hurt me but to help me cross the finish line.

"It's one of the reasons I surrounded myself with all the swag from the army recruiters. Seeing all this stuff reminding me that my future is coming made my classes not seem so hopeless. When I'm in class, either in person or digitally, I see all this army stuff and know just being in class will help me get there. Changing the way I see school from being hurtful to helpful made the work easier. Don't get me wrong, I will still be super glad when the plague ends and school goes back to normal, but even if it doesn't this year, I'll be okay."

My son's actions highlight the power of appraisal. The way we think impacts the way we feel and the amount of willpower we have in a given situation. Reframing the way we see things is a powerful strategy for students. Appraisal gives a person control in any circumstance, no matter how grim. When conditions can't be altered, it's always possible to change the way we think.

RESPONSE STRATEGIES

The last strategy is just to use willpower. This strategy is employed when a person forces themselves to do something despite temptations. This strategy is the worst-case scenario because actively using will to sustain work causes fatigue and negative feelings that can perpetuate burnout. It's one of the reasons Dr. Inzlicht compares willpower to an emergency brake. It can work temporarily to get you through a tough spot, but when used as a go-to strategy over and over, it can wear on a person and, with overuse, fail to work.

The good news is that using willpower in combination with the other strategies can help increase self-control and lower the chance of burnout. For instance, a person studying might use various strategies to prevent distraction. While they're studying, if their phone rings, they might appraise the call as not being that important. But then, as they turn their phone off, it pings, indicating a text message. They look again at their phone, but the precommitment app they downloaded to help them focus shuts down their ability to see the text and reminds them they have fifty more minutes of studying before they can read the message. They turn off the phone. Finally, when a friend walks by and waves for them to come out to talk, they shake their head and use willpower to keep going.

So which strategy helps the most? All of them. Dr. Inzlicht tested all of these strategies in a recent lab study and found that "they all seem to work more or less, but multiple strategies was the winner." The key to willpower is having multiple tools to use for the various temptations and situations that may arise.

Showcasing each strategy gives students a working toolbox they can use to strengthen their willpower. These strategies enable students to find the motivation to reach their goals and, as they do, build agency. It's been said that where there's a will, there's a way. The reality? Strategies support the will to make the way.

HELPFUL HABITS

Although not a strategy, forming habits can impact willpower and increase the likelihood of reaching a goal. A habit requires willpower initially but over time requires little will as it becomes a natural, ingrained tendency. All the self-control strategies can work to support the formation of habits.

Mary didn't originally realize that her precommitment would turn into the habit of studying with her friend nightly. Habits change the amount of energy we expend. After studying at her friend's house for a few weeks, Mary mentioned that she was studying on autopilot. She felt this way because habits are the brain's way to save energy by making repetitive tasks more efficient. Mary's habit formed out of the cues she used nightly. The ritual time of 7:00 p.m. cued Mary to get out her study materials and contact her friend. By creating an implementation intention to study with her friend at 7:00, she allowed the time to automatically cue her brain to study.[12] Through the use of cues, repetition, and positive reinforcement, small positive behaviors can turn into habits.

Talking to her friend also offered Mary a built-in reward for fulfilling the habit of working on homework. Without knowing it, she created a perfect storm to form a habit. The positive reinforcement built a positive feedback loop that supported the behavior and ritual to turn into a habit.

Students can use cues, appraisals, and rewards as tools to form a new habit. The cue provides a starting point for the action to happen. Appraisal supplies the motivation to act by making the action tempting. The reward reinforces the desire to complete the action again, creating an incentive to keep repeating the process.

According to research, on average, it takes more than two months for a new behavior to become automatic.[13] Habits depend on the behavior, the person, and the circumstances. To create ripe circumstances for a habit to form, students should define their motivation, create a clear cue, use appraisals to make the actions more enticing, and, lastly, use reward to make the effort of their actions worth it.

Creating good habits can help us function more efficiently and save our willpower. On top of that, the habits we form, whether good or bad, ultimately shape who we become. If a person has a habit of practicing gratitude, they'll become a happier person, or if a person eats vegetables with each meal, they will become a healthier person. The habits students form can set them up to lead a happy, healthy life despite obstacles they might encounter

We know bad days will happen. On those days where we may not feel like exerting effort, habits can make all the difference. Exercising, eating well, or working can help us strive towards goals even when we don't feel like it. When storms hit, we have a foundation of positive behaviors that can see us through.

TAKING THE TIME

Sometimes struggles steal the life from us. Habits, strategies, and willpower can keep us going. Willpower strategies offer simple methods to resist temptations and boost agency. Habits help us automatically keep doing actions despite circumstances. Through fighting small battles of will, students see that they control and can change outcomes. In a moment of struggle, this could be the difference between a kid giving up or giving it their all.

Willpower is a struggle for all of us, and those with high willpower use strategies and habits regularly to reach their goals. Strategies can help students with low agency find the motivation and belief to achieve their goals. If we want students to persevere, we need to teach them how to do so. Modeling these strategies may take a couple of days, but their impact can last a lifetime.

HEART TO HEART

QUESTIONS AND IDEAS FOR ACTION

Reflect, discuss with a group, or share your thoughts and create a dialogue on social media using the book's hashtag, #HOPEforEdu.

Questions

1. When faced with distractions and temptations, what strategies do you use to keep going? How could you use your example to help students with their willpower?

2. What's something that distracts you from your goals? What strategy or strategies could you use to help avoid getting distracted? Why do you think it's essential to share struggles and strategies with students as they learn to build willpower?

Ideas for Action

- Research precommitment websites, apps, and computer extensions. Create a list of precommitment tools and try some out to increase your willpower. Consider sharing the list with students or colleagues.

- Try a mindfulness meditation via YouTube or through a mindfulness app. Compare your feelings before and after use on a sheet of paper. What did you notice? What did you feel?

- Think of something that you must do that might be draining your willpower. Write it down. Now try reappraisal to think about the task and how you might do it differently. How could you reframe it? Keep that thought in mind when you must do the task and see how it impacts your energy and will.

INFUSING MOTIVATION AND WILLPOWER

A person's willpower or agency is a complex mix of intrinsic motivation, physical energy, and extrinsic forces. Each piece of the willpower puzzle is vital to consider when developing a person's willpower and agency. It's a matter of working with different combinations to find what works for a person.

Multiple research studies have tested various intrinsic and extrinsic components that impact willpower, and they all boil down to perception. Our will evolves in sync with the perception of the resources that we have available to us. Your mind looks at the resources it has, such as food, social supports, and tools, to decide how much energy it can exert at a given time. The more resources, the safer we feel expending energy because we know we have the means to fill back up when depleted. With time, our emotions evolved to respond positively in moments of plenty and negatively in times of want. That's one of the reasons we feel like we can do more when we feel positive than when we feel negatively.[14]

The strength of various factors can change the difficulty a person perceives a task to have. Through checking in and meeting the needs of students, offering social support, and purposefully increasing students' positive perception of a task, we can boost intrinsic drive and improve the hope and outcomes for our students.

MOTIVATION AND NEEDS

Boosting willpower and student agency starts with making sure students feel their needs are met. In research studies, psychologists put various people in front of a hill and asked them to estimate the slant of the hill. Since the researchers just wanted an estimate, you would think that people would get close to the correct answer. You might also presume the pattern of the guesses they made would be random. The reality is the studies revealed that certain factors impact how we see the world.

In one test, the researchers gave one group of people perceiving the hill a glass of sugar water and another group a glass of normal water.[15] The group with the sugar water perceived the hill as less steep and more manageable than the first group. In another study, the researchers found that people in more positive moods perceived the hill as less steep than those in negative ones.[16] Other factors that impacted perception included age, how physically fit a person was, if they had a friend nearby, and how refreshed a person felt.[17,18]

This research doesn't mean we should go around adding sugar to our water fountains! It means that before a person works on a more challenging goal, we need to make sure they feel okay and have their basic needs met. Chapter 2 showed how a mental health check-in form can serve as a preventative measure to catch problems. That same form also helps with differentiating the motivational needs of your students for the day.

When you view the check-in forms, any student who indicates that they are just feeling okay and making it through may need more motivation for the day.

Educators can help promote agency in three specific ways: reminding students of their purpose for setting goals, adding options and pathways for social support, and building intrinsic motivation into classroom lessons.

Defining Motivation

In Chapter 4, when Wilson defined his long-term goal to help his grandma beat cancer using the pathway milestones tool, the last question prompted him to write down why his goal was crucial. Remembering the importance of a task can motivate a person when they become less motivated. Often when a person works on a larger goal, it's easy to forget why they set the goal in the first place. Going back to the foundational level of why the task is essential reminds a person of their desire that formed the goal in the first place.

Sometimes defining a student's motivation for a task involves some digging. The pathway miletones tool involves a personal desire or passion. With the daily goals they set and the routines they must follow, it's easy for students to become muddled with what they have to do and forget why they started a task in the first place. A simple way to help students who may need an extra boost is prompting them to remember the reason they are doing a task, activity, or goal.

I use a simple question to help students reframe *have to* moments into *want to* moments: How could this help the future you? By defining its motivation in the present, we can help reframe a task to be more lucrative and, with this, increase motivation. Sometimes it involves asking the question multiple times to lead students to define their motivation, but the more they connect it to their end purpose, the more motivation they gain for the task.

For example, Wilson, who had trouble with initial goal setting, needed to think about this question so he could develop the motivation to push through stuck moments as he grew his pathways score. It took a lot of agency for him to work on his pathways. His strength of will helped him develop his pathways by defining his motivation for a task. For example, one day he had a math assignment that was particularly difficult for him. As he entered the room, he said, "These five homework questions are going to take forever!"

I replied, "True, it might take a while, but how could this help the future you?"

"I guess it could help future me get a good grade."

Notice that a good grade could be someone's motivation, but it's not defining the actual reason to keep pushing. The further we can get someone to explain their reason for doing something, the deeper their motivation will be. So I reframed the question and asked again.

"How could a good grade help the future you?"

"Well, it could help me get into the welding program I want to take."

"How could that help future you?"

"I would get to live my dream and help my family. I wish my parents didn't have to work so hard, so it would help them."

He then put the paper away. Later that day, I saw him working on it at lunch. Sometimes when we remind ourselves of our motivation, it provides enough boost to tackle complex tasks.

Building Positive Affect

According to research, students' moods, emotions, and overall dispositions impact their work, decision-making, and self-control. Studies on affect or emotions have found that stimulating positive feelings can increase self-control and stop ego depletion.[19,20] Building an environment infused with mood-boosting opportunities and stimuli will increase students' intrinsic motivation to help them thrive.

Think about how your mood impacts the work you do. Recall a time when you felt happy or satisfied in the workplace. How did it impact your work and effort? According to research, positive affect or emotion boosted your productivity and your willpower at that moment. In the brain, positive emotions decrease the stress hormone cortisol and increase serotonin and dopamine feel-good chemicals in the brain. Serotonin and dopamine promote physical and emotional safety. So not only does working actively to promote positive affect improve willpower, it also helps with safety and trust so students will feel supported while learning to master content.

Students' emotions are integral to their safety, the work they do, and the self-control they have. Every student brings their emotions to school. Those emotions drive performance and with it drive feelings for other people. Each student is an emotion conductor, and it's up to us to infuse the positive so they can pass it around.

Infusing positive affect or emotions can be done with simple practices that take minimal time but that significantly impact student mood and classroom culture. Interweaving routines such as using humor, practicing positive reflection, and teaching positive self-talk promote positive emotions and assist students to develop more positive mindsets.

Humor

Humor can improve student emotions and, according to research, help them remember what they learn.[21] When we find something funny, we tend to pay closer attention to what is happening, causing us to retain information better.[22] Humor can be used quickly to boost the mood in a lesson, and the educational impact of using it is enormous. Humor can also help teachers teach content more effectively, improve the mood and drive of students, and build student interest. The key is to make sure the humor coincides with content, is not offensive, and is used sporadically to focus students' attention on critical components of a lesson.

There are various ways teachers could infuse humor in a lesson. A teacher might start class with a humorous comic strip or joke about the content to help illustrate a point. A teacher could use a funny story to highlight something important in a lesson or emphasize an issue. Humorous mnemonics could also lighten a lesson and help students remember critical steps or information, such as when my students learned the research mnemonic CRAAP to use in the evaluation of sources. As soon as students see the mnemonic, they chuckle, and the evaluation steps stick with them throughout the year.

Positive Reflection

At the end of class, instead of just ending with an exit ticket or activity, give students thirty to forty seconds to reflect on one positive thing that happened during the period. Students could write down their positive reflections or share them out loud. The point is to get students into the practice of reflecting on the good.

Practicing positive reflection can foster students' brains to develop neural pathways that focus on and look for the positive in their day. Over time this practice can encourage students to develop more positive mindsets. Positive reflection takes only seconds, but repeating the exercise over time can help students see how what they focus on impacts their overall feelings and mental health.

Searching for the positive can also assist students to change the negative thoughts that run through their minds about themselves and their abilities. Due to trauma or other events, many students have developed harmful scripts that impact their self-esteem. They walk around daily thinking things such as, *I suck at this. I'm no good. No one cares about me.*

Negative thoughts can contribute to feelings of hopelessness and low agency, which impacts willpower, so it's essential to provide students with examples of positive self-talk. Including positive cause-and-effect feedback on assignments can promote students to generate positive self-talk. Teachers can use posters, messages written on a board, and empowering feedback to get students to see and use positive self-talk.

Posters that showcase a growth mindset can help students see how to correct negative self-talk. Also, highlighting the positive aspects of a student's work can help them see how their efforts have impact. For instance, writing, "You did a great job using details to make your point in this paragraph" helps the student see that they are good at writing details and that their efforts matter.

Fostering a learning environment that instills positive emotions supports willpower and student learning, safety, and well-being. Positive emotions feel good, and they're good for students. Humor, positive reflection, and the fostering of positive self-talk can infuse students with determination when they struggle. Taking the time to incorporate positive emotions in the classroom will boost intrinsic motivation. Over time, practicing positivity can lead to students developing a habit of it, which helps them become happier people.

Social Support

Access to social resources also impacted a person's perception in the hill experiment. The more social support a person perceived, the lower the slant of the hill seemed to them. In the classroom, that translates to the more social help we offer to students, the more motivation and energy they will have for activities, tasks, or assignments. The hope mentors and partners in the learning goal cycle act as one form of social support, but we must have additional tools to provide support when a student feels unmotivated.

One great way to provide social support for students is by asking parents and guardians to provide a letter of encouragement to their students. Ask a parent to e-mail words of support for a day their child might feel unmotivated. If a student's guardian chooses not to send in a letter, you could ask other teachers or people in the school building to write a supportive message. Once you receive the words of support, keep them and use them when a student shows low motivation or needs encouragement. It will give them a motivation boost and make them perceive what's going on in front of them as less intimidating, reducing the size of the metaphorical hill before them.

The hill experiment also found that sometimes just reminding a person of their social support increased positive perception. When a student struggles with motivation, sometimes having them create a list of people who believe in them is enough to remind them of the relationships that matter, thus shifting their perception of the task in front of them. Thinking of people who believe in you helps to increase your belief in yourself. Often our minds blow moments out of proportion. Grounding your motivation with a reminder of the love and support around you makes things feel less intimidating and decreases the hill.

Having a bragging rights card can also help cue students into their social supports and act as a means of extrinsic positive reinforcement. The card does not have to be complicated. It could have spaces for the student's name, who they want to brag to, and what they did. Copy a set of bragging rights cards and offer them to students who seem they might need extra motivation. Any student should be able to access the cards, but take the time to specifically remind those who may be struggling to fill out a card.

All you have to do is take a picture of the card and e-mail it if the recipient is a parent or guardian, or, if the child chooses a friend, they can take the card with them and deliver it personally. The practice takes hardly any time at all but reminds students of their social supports. It also allows the child to highlight a positive part of their day and receive recognition from a person they value, reminding them there are people in their corner just waiting to cheer them on.

Increasing Intrinsic Motivation

Self-determination theory, created by Dr. Edward Deci and Dr. Richard Ryan, lists three key components for increasing intrinsic motivation and agency: competence, autonomy, and relatedness. Increasing intrinsic motivation in

FIGURE 5.4 BRAGGING RIGHTS

To: From:

I have bragging rights!

Just a little note to say today I:

everyday activities provides greater satisfaction and engagement for students in the classroom. It also ensures higher success rates as you are interweaving motivation students can use to succeed in lessons, projects, and activities.

When schools focus on building practices that increase intrinsic motivation, they drive students to engage in their learning, and, as students engage, they excel. Building intrinsic motivation into a lesson is just a matter of analyzing the pieces of the lesson for ways that competence, autonomy, and relatedness can be applied in the activities.

Educators can easily sit down with their lessons and use the built-in lesson engagement planner tool in Figure 5.6 to see the level of intrinsic motivation interwoven within a task. The more an activity covers one of the aspects of self-determination theory, the more engagement the activity provides; for example, instead of assigning a reading by simply offering a choice, the lesson shifts to give a point in the autonomy category and boosts the intrinsic motivation built into the activity. This planning tool helps educators check for and build in components that will support student intrinsic motivation and engagement.

Once we understand the components of competence, autonomy, and relatedness, we can craft lessons that meet our students' motivational needs and create activities and practices that fuel every student's drive to learn and engage.

FIGURE 5.5   THREE BASIC INTRINSIC MOTIVATION NEEDS

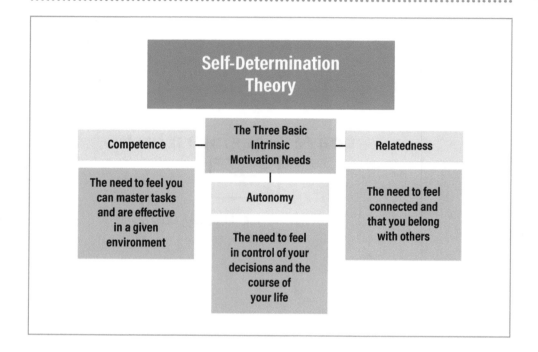

Competence

Competence is feeling effective in your environment and believing you have the right skills to complete a task. Think of the last time someone praised you for a skill or idea. It might have been a thank you note from a student, or a random note of appreciation from your boss. How did it make you feel? I'm sure it felt great! When you look at this closely, it did more than make you feel good. When people feel like they impact their environment and are effective, it increases their intrinsic motivation and boosts hopeful agency. It's a feeling that your unique skills and perspective are valued and challenged in an environment. To increase competence in schools, students need the opportunity to respond to and contribute to their learning.

There are multiple ways to support a student's competence and provide them with challenges to increase their skill level. You might consider the one-to-two rule in which you give the students two minutes of active response and engagement to show their competence for every minute of instruction. The two minutes could consist of open-ended questions to the class, a Jamboard to post students' thoughts online, or the chance to work with a partner or group to discuss or apply manipulatives based on what is being learning. Taking the time to seek out and ask for student input signals to students that they are valued and boosts intrinsic motivation in the classroom.

If I know I will need ten minutes to present a concept to students, they should get twenty minutes of competence time interwoven into that lesson at some

FIGURE 5.6 LESSON PLAN

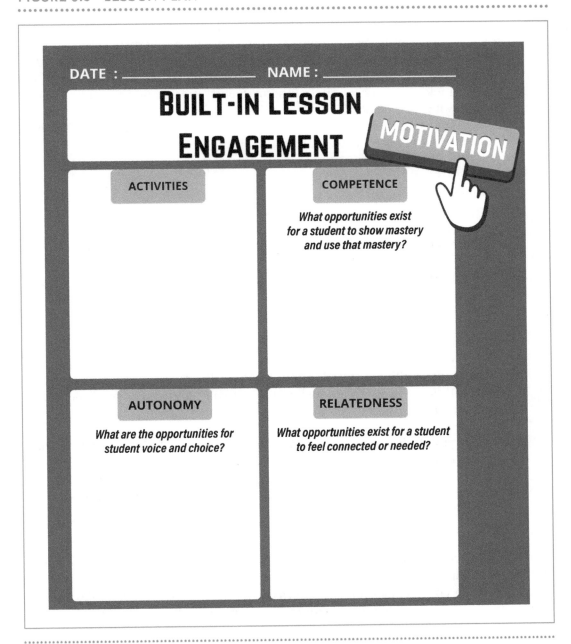

BUILT-IN LESSON ENGAGEMENT MOTIVATION

DATE : _____ NAME : _____

ACTIVITIES

COMPETENCE

What opportunities exist for a student to show mastery and use that mastery?

AUTONOMY

What are the opportunities for student voice and choice?

RELATEDNESS

What opportunities exist for a student to feel connected or needed?

SOURCE: Based on the work of Ryan, R. M., & Deci, E. L. (2000). Self-determination theory and the facilitation of intrinsic motivation, social development, and well-being. *American Psychologist, 55*(1), 68–78. https://doi.org/10.1037/0003-066x.55.1.68

point. It is important that the students must have more competence time than I do. Teachers are already competent in their subject area. Students need this time to prove that they are capable and gain the intrinsic joy of understanding a concept.

This simple time split also shows that you value student competence above your own. When someone lectures to you about a skill or presents a talk, it might be entertaining or even enlightening, but are you part of the learning? Do you personally feel valued in their ramblings? This simple time rule ensures that the student is part of the process—that their thoughts, ideas, and "a-ha" moments matter. Plus, as they share their unique perspectives and ideas on a subject, sometimes they stumble upon ways to help other students understand the content better than how it was presented in the lesson. Students have value to add to all lessons, and making sure they feel that their skills and strengths are used in a learning partnership boosts competence and intrinsic motivation.

Autonomy

Everyone wants to feel in control of their environment. Control is a crucial piece in motivating students to engage, and lack of control is demotivating. Just think of the last time you were told you *had* to do something. Go to this meeting. Take out the trash. Write this letter. Even if the desire to do the task was there initially, you become unmotivated as soon as you get told that you *must* do something. Everyone has certain things they have to do, but the more we give students choices in the things they have to do, the more those *have to* tasks can transform into *want to* tasks.

Autonomy provides students the opportunity to make choices and have a say in their learning. Adding autonomy gives students the ability to mesh what they are learning with their understanding of the world. Increasing school autonomy starts with looking at the amount of student voice and choice provided in any given activity.

Voice gives a student a say in their learning and acknowledges their backgrounds, perspectives, opinions, and beliefs. Instead of telling students they have to do a specific activity or lesson to gain mastery, create a way to propose their learning path. Passion projects and activities such as Genius Hour allow students a voice in their learning. Giving students a say in their education gives them control and motivation to learn and master classroom material.

Adding choice looks at increasing the amount of decision-making power a person has in a given task. Instead of limiting students to one activity and just offering voice, consider providing choices as to how they learn the material. You could do this by simply giving them more than one way to do an assignment, or you could offer choice boards that allow students options for how they practice and use the material. Just making sure that students have options in a given lesson increases engagement. Students can use choice boards to choose how to learn a concept, which boosts their intrinsic motivation and hope.

Relatedness

Why do we form families? Or seek out friendships? Or try to find a workplace where we are valued and needed? Relatedness is a person's innate need to feel connected to and belonging with others. Everyone wants to feel that they matter to someone. When this need is met, we try harder and push more because we believe our contributions assist those we love.

Providing opportunities for students to be involved with partners or groups that require various skill sets and talents helps children feel valued and needed by their peers. For example, offering students group work that gives them a chance to choose a role or skill set to show their learning increases the students' feeling of belonging in the group. This type of rich group work involves each child contributing a piece to the larger whole of the group.

Another method to increase relatedness is using jigsawing. In jigsawing students learn components of a lesson and then move to another group to share the expertise they learned from the first group. In a jigsaw group, students work together in two phases. In the first phase, groups of "experts" work together to learn information on a specialized topic related to the lesson. In the second phase, the expert groups split up and reform into "generalist" groups containing one representative from each former expert group.

For example, when studying geometric areas in math, one expert group might learn how to calculate the area of a square. Once they understand that component, they diverge from their expert group to join a general group where they share information and learn from other groups' experts on calculating the area of a circle, triangle, parallelogram, and trapezoid. Each student is a needed and crucial expert in the general group, increasing intrinsic motivation and student engagement.

In addition to activities, we can convey relatedness in the words we use with students. A simple tactic, for example, is to speak of "we" and "us" as much as possible rather than saying "you students." Another tactic is to create moments of partnership learning between you as the educator and the student. Instead of telling students how a strategy tool works or what a lesson means, ask them to work with you and with each other to define what they have learned. Having students highlight the central ideas or points in a lesson using partnership learning helps them relate to you and the other students as you work together to recap a lesson or activity. Also, using the learning goal cycle in class works to strengthen student competence, autonomy, and relatedness. The more ways we work to increase hope, the more we grow our students' chances of success.

Ultimately, interweaving intrinsic motivation components into a student's day gives them extra power to reach and achieve their goals, thus boosting their agency. Increasing agency is not a matter of attempting every practice in this chapter. Any step you take to help a child grow hope is impactful. You might just do one or two things. The important part is to start measuring, analyzing, and boosting hope. You do that today, you change a child's tomorrow. Building positive beliefs and attributions. Building goals. Building pathways. Building agency. Building hope. Giving students the power to fight tomorrow's battles, push past barriers, and accomplish more than they ever possibly imagined.

Hope can keep us going when we feel like everything is falling apart so our life, goals, and future fall into place.

FIGURE 5.7   AGENCY DO'S AND DON'TS

Fostering Agency and Willpower to Increase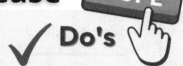

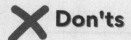 Don'ts

- **Don't** tell kids to push through and just rely on their willpower.

- **Don't** discount students' feelings and the power their mood has on their learning.

- **Don't** assume students know how to develop habits and why habits are important.

- **Don't** dwell on failures of will or concentrate on negative moments.

- **Don't** plan lessons without providing components for the diverse motivational needs of your students.

✓ Do's

- **Do** teach students different strategies to use with their willpower.

- **Do** plan lessons that will foster positive emotions in students to support their learning and willpower.

- **Do** teach students how habits form and how they can use habits to reach their goals.

- **Do** teach students to focus on the positive and their growth.

- **Do** purposefully plan time in lessons to meet students' feelings of competence, autonomy, and relatedness.

 **HEART TO HEART**

QUESTIONS AND IDEAS FOR ACTION

Reflect, discuss with a group, or share your thoughts and create a dialogue on social media using the book's hashtag, #HOPEforEdu.

Questions

1. How do you gain motivation when you feel unmotivated? How could you use your answer to help build agency for your students?

2. Why do you feel it's essential to define a person's motivation before they pursue a goal? How would defining why you are doing something help you accomplish the goal? Do you feel it's essential to clarify why you teach students content, rules, or expectations? How could this help your school build student motivation?

Ideas for Action

- Think of something that sucks away student motivation. It could be a school or classroom rule, procedure, or activity. Use the tools of helping students define motivation, utilizing social support, and building in the components of intrinsic motivation to change the motivator sucker into a motivation infuser. Show others how you used what you learned to increase agency and, with it, increase hope for students.

Energizing: Building Hopeful Cultures

It is easy to fall into learned helplessness in the school environment due to the lack of hope. I call this lack of hope the optimism gap. It occurs when educators day in and day out are forced to focus and combat the negative, such as a lack of resources, mandated testing, or discipline issues. When a mind gets conditioned only to look and react to a few negative things, it prevents us from seeing the good. Just as educators need to help students build hope, organizations need to find ways to increase hope and optimism for staff. Hopeful cultures are necessary to promote hopeful employees who can mentor and foster hope in their students.

The work to instill hope in schools starts by filling the optimism gap and rewiring cultures to concentrate on strengths instead of weaknesses. We work hard in schools to manage behavior and expectations, but it takes more work to address the positive. Building a hopeful culture cannot be achieved with a one-time reward, an employee of the month recognition, or even a shout-out; it starts with building practices to improve the outlook and motivation of staff. Self-determination theory can foster the beginning of this process by increasing the relatedness, autonomy, and competence every colleague experiences within their roles.

Many of these practices are little things that add to the culture and over time fill the optimism gap. These practices build competence, autonomy, relatedness, and, most importantly, hope. It's not just a top-down approach, this is a culture shift, and everyone has to get on board to fill in the gap to create a culture of happiness, satisfaction, and hope.

Every person matters in a school culture, and it's the small contributions that we all make that create the culture we share. What can you do to improve the outlook and motivation of staff? The suggestions here are not a limited resource. Your contribution matters in this conversation. That's why it's imperative we share what works, what tools we use, and the things we do to support educators in various staff rooms throughout the country so they feel cared for and loved. One culture of hope can spread to another.

Samples of Success

To boost teacher and staff competence, staff members should compile samples of success throughout a month or quarter. Grade-level teams or departments could hold each other accountable for taking the time to gather samples of success. The goal is not only to collect the samples but also to display them to showcase the small wins. Samples could include e-mails from family members, a lesson a teacher is proud of, or a student work sample. You are only limited by what you define as *success*. The point of the samples is that gathering them intentionally forces us to look for the good in our day to day. The wins might be small, but any win matters. This practice promotes competence and relatedness in an organization.

Most importantly, administrators should give teachers time to display and talk about their samples of success. Promoting positive dialogue on ideas can inspire lessons, lead to new support strategies for students, or even just result in a pat on the back for a job well done. It is one more thing being added to everyone's plate, but when the plate tends to look empty, samples of success provide some nourishment.

Difference-Maker Meetings

A study from 2009 on attracting and retaining teachers found that one of the key motivational factors for a teacher choosing to leave is when they feel they are not making a difference.[1] This idea of working hard repeatedly but feeling that your efforts are meaningless can cause negative attributions and learned helplessness for staff. To help school staff focus on their effectiveness, you can have them use and implement the difference-maker meeting rule.

Before any meeting, whether team, grade level, or department, every staff member should be given a minute to talk about a kid they feel they have connected to and impacted. These discussions help school cultures in two key ways: They provide a bright spot to mandatory meetings, and they give each staff member a chance to think about their impact.

Ending on a Positive Note

The optimism gap can have the most significant ramification on the way we remember our day. One student's behavior can cause a staff member or administrator to define their day as a catastrophe. The way we begin and end a day helps explain how our memory represents and encodes that day. If the focus is the one bad thing, it will be one of the only things you will be able to recall the next day.

To help decrease the gap and promote a more well-rounded perception of the day, encourage staff to use the activity Ending on a Positive Note. Take the time to think of one student who deserves some praise. Write an e-mail or call that kid's home and let their guardians know about the student's success. This helps educators form positive relationships with guardians and students and reminds them that there are still rays of light even when a day seems dark.

Hope Makers

If your school has any sort of student recognition process or awards ceremony, you can add a simple practice to what's already in place to remind staff members of their impact. Often we reward students but forget to reward the people who helped them on their path to success.

To recognize the impact staff members make and increase students' voices, add an opportunity for students to identify a staff member who contributed to their success. Doing this could happen at the end of a student recognition ceremony by asking them to write a quick thank you note to a staff member they feel contributed to their success, or kids could be given a moment to say the name of a staff member who helped them be successful. This activity teaches kids to show gratitude, reminds students of social support, empowers staff, and reminds staff why we go to school each day: to see kids find their success.

The little things we do each day work to build a culture. Creating a culture of optimism can be an instrumental first step toward significant and lasting improvement in schools. These practices are small but impactful. Culture can drain us or infuse us. To make staff feel empowered, needed, and hopeful, we must safeguard against the optimism gap. When a school culture is focused on the positive empowerment of staff, educators can see how they make a difference, which causes them to feel valued. People who feel their voice and work are valued are not likely to leave. Infusing teachers with motivation helps them reach the ultimate goal of why most educators go into education: to make a difference every day for every kid.

CHAPTER 6

THE SCHOOL OF HOPE

WHEN THE WORLD LOST ITS MIND

Fear. Panic. Isolation. I open my computer to the gentle ping of chat messages in the background. Within seconds the pinging becomes a solid cascade of beeps making audible music, and thirty-five messages appear on my Gmail screen. It's been three days since the governor decided school would close for the year. The messages are varied, but they all share a similar thread of panic, insecurity, and confusion.

"No school? Does that mean we still do the project?"

"My mom can't find toilet paper. Can you help, Mrs. B.?"

"Is this like a snow day? But with a virus?"

"My dad's store has to close. What's going to happen to me?"

"Umm . . . could this kill me?"

"I *can't* be locked in a house with my family."

"Do you have masks? The hospital ran out. Mom says it's a war zone. She's reused the same mask for three days."

"My ma's travel company fired her. They said travel's out. What if we lose our house?"

"The news said schools closed for the rest of the year—that's like months. Why?!"

"I feel scared. I feel it all the time. I wake up scared. How do I make it go away?"

"Grocery shelves are empty. A woman pushed my abuela to the floor because my abuela wouldn't let go of diapers for my baby brother. *She's an old woman!* The world's lost its mind."

Even though they are panicking, I am relieved to hear from these students. It means they can connect with others to seek support and talk about their feelings. But what of the other forty students who haven't sent messages? I e-mail, I call, I reach out. Silence.

Nearly two years later, after virtual, hybrid, and canceled learning, students are mostly back in classrooms. The only difference? Emotions weigh down the staff and students; instead of jumping for joy, the weight drags their steps. The emotions are as varied as the faces: trauma, anger, sadness, depression, and anxiety from waiting for the next disaster to hit.

School was reliable and safe until it came to a standstill, making even the mightiest of us experience fear and question what would happen next. The emotions students now carry cause some to cry or overreact to common classroom stimuli. Others express themselves with disruptive behavior. Among adolescents, the emotional weight of the pandemic has brought increased violence, destructive TikTok challenges, and a rise in bullying.

Some, however, try to keep their fear and sadness bottled up. A typical school day that would once be easy quickly becomes too much. They don't know how to tell anyone that these feelings just won't go away.

In October 2021, the American Academy of Pediatrics, the Children's Hospital Association, and the American Academy of Child and Adolescent Psychiatry declared a national state of emergency due to declines in child and adolescent mental health related to the pandemic.[1] The declaration cited that the stress of COVID-19 and ongoing struggles for racial justice have impacted child and adolescent mental health. A steady rise in mental health concerns and suicide among children has occurred within the past ten years, and recent events have only made the situation worse. It's time to build in supports to take back the mental health and well-being of our children.

For me, this book and its subject matter are personal. I know trauma impacts children. As you've read, my own children lived through horrendous abuse and neglect. To help them, I scoured the Internet and scholarly databases and talked with mental health professionals about what I could do. Then one research article changed the trajectory of my journey to help my children: *Camp HOPE as an Intervention for Children Exposed to Domestic Violence: A Program Evaluation of Hope, and Strength of Character.* It explained how Camp HOPE America measured and used hope as an intervention and coping resource for campers with adverse childhood experiences.

The results of measuring and strengthening hope were astounding: improved grit, self-control, optimism, gratitude, social intelligence, and curiosity. And reports of the positive outcomes from hope weren't isolated to this study. A quick scholarly search on the impact of hope yielded many other articles, including:

- *Hope as a Mediator of Bullying Involvement and Emotional Difficulties in Children*
- *Psychosocial Perceptions and Executive Functioning: Hope and School Belonging Predict Students' Executive Functioning*
- *How Hope Measures Up: Hope Predicts School Variables beyond Growth Mindset and School Belonging*
- *A Potential Avenue for Academic Success: Hope Predicts an Achievement-Oriented Psychosocial Profile in African American Adolescents*
- *Hope into Action: How Clusters of Hope Relate to Success-Oriented Behavior in School*
- *Dimensions of Hope in Adolescence: Relations to Academic Functioning and Well-Being*
- *The Magic of Hope: Hope Mediates the Relationship between Socioeconomic Status and Academic Achievement*

So learning about, measuring, and strengthening hope became my focus. Through thousands of hours of research, interviews, and the attainment of a master's degree in psychology, I built tools and practices focused on strengthening hope, all for the love of my children.

I knew from the research that measuring and strengthening hope could help at school too. The tools and practices that helped my own children could be remodeled to fit the demands of schools and the classroom. Before starting your journey to use hope, you might have the same questions I did:

- Is teaching and using hope worth my time?
- Is it able to be interwoven into schools and classrooms?
- Is it able to battle the psychological effects of a pandemic?
- Is it really going to impact school culture?

The answer to all these questions is yes. I used hope with my children to give them their best shot, and now I use it with my students and colleagues to do the same. The greatest part? By starting on this journey, you can make hope spread to students, friends, family, your community, and even to people you've never met.

You see, hope is contagious. A longitudinal study done in 2008 by Nicholas Christakis and Stephen Fowler found that emotional stampedes run through our social circles, shaping everything from the choices we make to the way we feel to the goals we set for our future.[2] They discovered that one person's emotions could impact up to three degrees of separation. This means that your hope level impacts not only you but also your friends, their friends, and the friends of your friends.

Now here is where the research done by Christakis and Fowler gets interesting: A person's hope depends on the people they are connected to. According to their study, people surrounded by hope in a social circle are more likely to become hopeful in the future. That means if we surround ourselves with hope, we can influence the outskirts of our social networks to have hope too. This is about more than just a student or staff gaining hope; it's about creating *schools of hope*. This is about building an educational network of hope that could have ripple effects on our communities, cities, and the world. That ripple starts with you.

SHOW HOPE IN ACTION

To help spread hope, people need to see and experience it. You can spread hope by modeling and showcasing it to others outside of using the tools and practices mentioned earlier in this book. The hope mentors discussed in Chapter 3 work on this principle; they have high hope and that hope works as a model to help others pick up hopeful practices and ways to think. Just taking the time to highlight the setting of goals, the planning of pathways, and the achievement of agency can help others become hopeful.

When we look to showcase hope, we don't have to rely just on ourselves. When the pandemic hit and school closed, the story of one teenage girl stuck in an apartment with her family became a model of hope and a beacon for my students.

After receiving an onslaught of messages when school closed, I decided to hold a daily digital class for those interested. It wouldn't count for a grade. It would just be a bit of consistency, learning, and socialization to help those who longed for something to cling to. On the first day, the students' mental health check-ins indicated their fear and worry. They wanted me to tell them things would be okay, even though the world wasn't. Instead, I decided to show them a model of hope by reading the play adaptation of *The Diary of Anne Frank*.

The students would log onto Google Meet for an hour every day, using phones or Wi-Fi or by dialing in. I made sure every student had a copy of the play. Through long pauses and lags on the Internet, they perserved and chose roles to read aloud. At first, they saw little in the story other than a girl whose plight reflected their own: Stuck inside. Family driving you crazy. Going outside could be deadly. However, as Anne started to highlight the beauty in her daily life, the students began to see some in their own. One student suggested we begin class by choosing one good thing from our day to model after Anne's journal entries. As we continued the story, Anne's modeled impact became greater.

In the end, as the Nazis drag Anne away to a fate of certain death, the story left the students with this quote from her diary: "In spite of everything, I still believe that people are really good at heart."

The students sat quietly.

Maggie, who had read the role of Anne, spoke after a moment. "I suppose she's right. We can choose to find hope even when things seem dark."

I asked them what we should do with our remaining time together. To that, Maggie responded, "Let's list the good in the pandemic."

Within seconds answers start filling the chat box:

- Time to sleep
- Family time!
- A newfound appreciation for toilet paper
- Stopping and enjoying the slowdown
- Realizing stuff doesn't matter, but people do
- Being grateful for school?
- Homemade tacos for lunch!
- Learning hope can be bigger than fear

The last comment struck a chord within me. Anne's story didn't change the pandemic for the students, but it did offer a model of hope in action. The hope from Anne's diary passed to the students and infused them with a renewed belief that the pandemic wouldn't define them. No matter what war, disease, or trials came their way, they could choose how to live. Anne isn't remembered because of the war but because of the hope she held and the person she became *despite* the war.

Stories like Anne's serve as guides in moments of struggle. When you overcome or use hope to find a way, it's important to share these victories so others can gain hope too. Taking the time to seek out and highlight hope is critical if we want others to find hope as well.

The more we highlight hope in our own lives and the lives of others, the more we spread hope. As a person learns from the hopeful social cues of others; they pick up key elements of hope, such as goals, pathways, and agency, and then they learn to model and spread hope too. Hope modeled and showcased with intentionality truly can change the world.

For the next month, consider seeking out one story of hope a day and sharing it with others. It could be your own experience, something you read, or something someone shares with you. As you do this, you'll notice something peculiar start to happen. Your brain will naturally begin to seek hope in the world, and it'll make a difference to those around you.

The stories will fill your corner of your social network with hope. Your purposeful tiny ripples will, over time, be noticed by those around you. Often negativity can be loud and grab our attention. We can't erase the negative, but we can blast hope so constantly and consistently that it becomes the background music we live our life to. And perhaps that music will be enough to help someone we don't know find some hope too.

PASS ALONG TOOLS AND SUPPORT OTHERS

Sharing stories of hope is one thing, but it's just as important to offer hope in the form of support for others. Often, we lack motivation (agency) or can't think of how to get past an obstacle (pathways), which can cause hope to dwindle. By helping others problem-solve past their barriers or find the motivation to reach their goals, you can help them find hope in a hard place.

This book highlights tools and practices to help in different situations where hope may dwindle. Don't think these tools are limited to just students. Share the tools and resources with friends and colleagues both inside and outside of school, and, most importantly, use your social network to highlight resources others can use. In addition to sharing hope-filled stories, consider letting people know about events and resources that exist in your own community.

The other day someone took a picture and posted about the splash pad and disk golf updates in my local community park. It might not seem like a big deal, but within minutes, many students and families had shared this post. This resource was invaluable for people looking for something to do and for students trying to find a safe place to have fun. You don't need to spotlight every resource, but when you pick up a movie from a library, get your taxes done for free, or find free babysitting through a local organization, take the time to let others know. You might be providing a resource that someone else needs right now that they didn't even know existed.

KEEP LEARNING AND SHARING

This book by no means is the only resource on hope. The key to improving hope in our schools, communities, and world is for all of us to keep learning and exploring the power of hope. As we discover more resources, tools, and strategies to improve our hope, we must share what we learn in order to contribute to the building of hope in others.

The hashtag #HOPEforEdu was created as a way for you to share what you learn and surround yourself with a hope-filled community so you have support, help, and a way to interact with each other. By learning and sharing, we can spark new ideas and discover new perspectives. Together we can strengthen hope and support others who come along to walk this journey with us.

To start you on this journey, I want to offer you a list of hopeful resources and people to learn from who can help you grow. This by no means is a definitive list but merely a starting point for you in your pursuit of deeper learning on hope.

Websites

- Beachboard, C. (2021, September). The School of HOPE. https://theschoolofhope.org/

- Houston, E. (2021, November 25). *What is hope in psychology + 7 exercises & worksheets*. PositivePsychology.com. https://positivepsychology.com/hope-therapy/

- Hopper, E. (2020, July 6). *The psychology of hope: How to build hope and a better future*. HealthyPsych.com. https://healthypsych.com/psychology-of-hope/

- Weir, K. (2013, October). *Mission impossible: Being hopeful is good for you—and psychologists' research is pinpointing ways to foster the feeling*. Monitor on Psychology. https://www.apa.org/monitor/2013/10/mission-impossible

- Wilkie, N., Shaw, B., Morgan, N., Cramoysan, S., Jones, L., Ding, K. S., Henry, A., Monk, S., & Jangra, P. (2021, November 18). *Home—the positive psychology people—positive psychology for everyone*. The Positive Psychology People. https://www.thepositivepsychologypeople.com/

- *The Journal of Positive Psychology*. Taylor & Francis. (n.d.). Retrieved November 28, 2021, from https://www.tandfonline.com/toc/rpos20/current

Books

- Lopez, S. J. (2014). *Making hope happen: Create the future you want for yourself and others*. Atria Paperback.

- Snyder, C. R. (1994). *The psychology of hope: You can get there from here*. Free Press.

- Gwinn, C., & Hellman, C. M. (2022). *Hope rising: How the science of hope can change your life*. Morgan James Publishing.

- Gallagher, M. W., & Lopez, S. J. (2018). *The Oxford Handbook of Hope*. Oxford University Press.

- Martin, A. (2016). *How we hope—a moral psychology*. Princeton University Press.

People to Learn From

- David B. Feldman

  https://www.davidfeldmanphd.com/podcastblog

  Facebook: https://www.facebook.com/DavidFeldmanPhD/

  Feldman is an associate professor of psychology at Santa Clara University. His research focuses on hope, meaning, and growth in the face of life's difficulties.

- Martin Seligman

  Twitter: @MartinEPSeligma

  https://www.coursera.org/specializations/positivepsychology

  Seligman is an American psychologist, educator, and author. Seligman is a strong promoter within the scientific community of positive psychology and well-being. He is also one of the founders of positive psychology.

- Ryan M. Niemiec

  Twitter: @ryanVIA

  https://www.viacharacter.org/about/people/ryan-niemiec

  An author, licensed psychologist, and educator, Niemiec serves as the education director of the VIA Institute on Character (www.viacharacter.org), a nonprofit organization in Cincinnati, where he leads workshops training practitioners around the world on the science and practice of character strengths.

- Barbara Fredrickson

  https://www.coursera.org/learn/positive-psychology

  https://www.authentichappiness.sas.upenn.edu/faculty-profile/barbara-l-fredrickson-phd

  Fredrickson is known for her broaden-and-build theory of positive emotions, which is foundational in positive psychology for guiding how pleasant emotional states contribute to resilience, well-being, and health.

A FINAL THOUGHT

As you take this journey, it's important to remember that every person is a work in progress. You wouldn't judge a story after reading a single word, or give your opinion on a cake after seeing only one ingredient. Instead, you would give the writer a chance to form several sentences or portray a thought before drawing conclusions on the story, or give the baker a chance to mix and bake the cake to form an opinion. Spreading, strengthening, and overhauling systems for hope takes time.

Give the writer time to write, the baker time to bake, and give hope time to flourish and take hold in your life and the lives of others. Hope is about agency and creating pathways towards goals, but as I've pointed out, it's also about the mindset we develop as we pay attention to the world around us.

One school might have many students who are actively involved in their education. Another might have tons of discipline referrals and only a single class of kids who show signs of engagement and success. Or, some students might excel at one school and then go to another and fail. Why? There are a lot of possible answers, but one key thing at the heart of each of these scenarios is that school administrators, teachers, and school staff make a difference.

I've been in a teacher's classroom where the hope is electrifying, where students smile, laugh, and share ideas as they set goals for their learning. I've watched a janitor stop and give advice to a kid in the hallway, turning a sour grimace into a grin as he points the kid to new pathways for his problems. I've been in buildings where administrators support the growth and goals of their people and hope feels like a tangible thing that can be touched. Hopeful people bring liveliness to their interactions with others. What does this show? It shows that no matter what position you're in, you and your hope matter.

Every person is born with hope. That's how this book started, and that's how it ends. Hope may fluctuate, and sometimes a person may need help to get it back, but we all have it. Some have more, and some have less, but we can ensure all people have enough hope to end up with positive life outcomes through purposeful measurement and practices.

Changing the world, changing school cultures, and changing classrooms starts with hope. It's a resource we can access in times of trial, and it can help us form a path where there is none. For those who've been through trauma and anxiety, hope can assist with healing and provide strength as they set goals for a brighter tomorrow.

We need you on this journey. The more we focus on strengthening and spreading hope, the more lives we can help. Your small stance to choose, model, and teach hope will be felt by those around you. You can help to build small pockets of hope that might bubble into a classroom of hope, faculties of hope, or maybe even a school of hope. Perhaps one day, with your help, every person on the planet will learn how to improve their hope and, with it, their lives—giving us seven billion reasons to have hope.

HEART TO HEART

QUESTIONS AND IDEAS FOR ACTION

Reflect, discuss with a group, or share your thoughts and create a dialogue on social media using the book's hashtag, #HOPEforEdu.

Questions

1. Has someone's perseverance ever made you go from feeling overwhelmed by a trial to believing you could overcome it? Who was that person and how did their story ease your mind or help you when you needed it? Why do you think it's important to showcase hope to others?

2. The social networks we surround ourselves with can be a powerful force to either increase or decrease hope in our lives. How can you purposefully increase the hope you see and interact with daily, whether online or in real life?

Ideas for Action

- Pick five people to encourage with a hopeful story or by sharing what you've learned about measuring and raising hope. List their names and what you will do to foster their hope.

- Start a revolution of hope. Perhaps start using hopeful practices with your colleagues. Maybe create your own pocket of hope in your classroom. Or possibly work together as administrators, teachers, staff, and students and take on the challenge to create a school of hope. Show. The. World. Share what you're doing by using the hashtag #HOPEforEdu. Model hope, teach hope, and, most importantly, spread hope.

REFERENCES/NOTES

CHAPTER 1: HOPE MAKERS

1. Snyder, C. (2002). Hope theory: Rainbows in the mind. *Psychological Inquiry, 13*(4), 249–275. http://jstor.org/stable/1448867

2. Blue Cross Blue Shield. (2021, May 20). *Data-driven healthcare.* The Health of America. https://www.bcbs.com/the-health-of-america

3. Debeic, J. (2018, September 24). Memories of trauma are unique because of how brains and bodies react to the threat. *The Conversation.* http://theconversation.com/memories-of-trauma-are-unique-because-of-how-brains-and-bodies-respond-to-threat-103725

4. Feeding America. (2019). *For people facing hunger, poverty is just one issue.* https://www.feedingamerica.org/hunger-in-america/facts

5. U.S Department of Housing and Urban Development. (2018). *Annual Homeless Assessment Report.* https://files.hudexchange.info/resources/documents/2018-AHAR-Part-1.pdf

6. U.S. Census Bureau. (2018). *Income and poverty in the United States: 2018.* https://www.census.gov/library/publications/2019/demo/p60-266.html

7. Psychology Today. (2021). *Trauma.* https://www.psychologytoday.com/us/basics/trauma

8. Felitti, V. J., Anda, R. F., Nordenberg, D., Williamson, D. F., Spitz, A. M., Edwards, V., Koss, M. P., & Marks, J. S. (1998). Relationship of childhood abuse and household dysfunction to many of the leading causes of death in adults. *American Journal of Preventive Medicine, 14*(4), 245–258. https://doi.org/10.1016/s0749-3797(98)00017-8

9. Stevens, J. E. (2017, April 25). *Nearly 35 million U.S. children have experienced one or more types of childhood trauma.* Aces Too High. https://acestoohigh.com/2013/05/13/nearly-35-million-u-s-children-have-experienced-one-or-more-types-of-childhood-trauma/

10. Møller, A. R. (2008). Neural plasticity: For good and bad. *Progress of Theoretical Physics Supplement, 173*, 48–65. https://doi.org/10.1143/ptps.173.48

11. Bremmer, J. D. (2006). Traumatic stress: Effects on the brain. *Dialogues in Clinical Neuroscience, 8*(4), 445–461. https://doi.org/10.31887/dcns.2006.8.4/jbremner

12. Bremmer, J. D. (2006). Traumatic stress: Effects on the brain. *Dialogues in Clinical Neuroscience, 8*(4), 445–461. https://doi.org/10.31887/dcns.2006.8.4/jbremner

13. Hawley, K. (2017). Trauma, trust, and time. *Psychology Today.* https://www.psychologytoday.com/us/blog/trust/201709/trauma-trust-and-time

CHAPTER 2: HEALING

1. Association for Psychological Science. (2007, August 28). We remember bad times better than good. *Science Daily.* www.sciencedaily.com/releases/2007/08/070828110711.htm

2. Forster, M., Gower, A. L., Borowsky, I. W., & McMorris, B. J. (2017). Associations between adverse childhood experiences, student-teacher

relationships, and non-medical use of prescription medications among adolescents. *Addictive Behaviors, 68*, 30–34. https://doi.org/10.1016/j.addbeh.2017.01.004

3. Bergin, C., & Bergin, D. (2009). Attachment in the classroom. *Educational Psychology Review, 21*(2), 141–170. https://doi.org/10.1007/s10648-009-9104-0

4. Brunzell, T., Waters, L., & Stokes, H. (2015). Teaching with strengths in trauma-affected students: A new approach to healing and growth in the classroom. *American Journal of Orthopsychiatry, 85*(1), 3–9. https://doi.org/10.1037/ort0000048

5. Fields, L., & Boccellari., A. (2017). *UC San Francisco Trauma Recovery Center Manual: A model for removing barriers to care and transforming services for survivors of violent crime.* Trauma Recovery Center. http://traumarecovery-center.org/trc-manual/

6. Herman, J. L. (1998). Recovery from psychological trauma. *Psychiatry and Clinical Neurosciences, 52*(S1). https://doi.org/10.1046/j.1440-1819.1998.0520s5s145.x

7. Miller, C. (2020, July 31). *How trauma affects kids in school.* Child Mind Institute. https://childmind.org/article/how-trauma-affects-kids-school/

8. Pennebaker, J. W., Kiecolt-Glaser, J. K., & Glaser, R. (1988). Disclosure of traumas and immune function: Health implications for psychotherapy. *Journal of Consulting and Clinical Psychology, 56*(2), 239–245. https://doi.org/10.1037/0022-006X.56.2.239

9. Child Welfare Information Gateway. (2014). *Parenting a child who has experienced trauma.* https://www.childwelfare.gov/pubs/factsheets/child-trauma/

10. Lim, B. H., Adams, L. A., & Lilly, M. M. (2012). Self-worth as a mediator between attachment and posttraumatic stress in interpersonal trauma. *Journal of Interpersonal Violence, 27*(10), 2039–2061. https://doi.org/10.1177/0886260511431440

11. Weisaeth, L. (1998). Vulnerability and protective factors for posttraumatic stress disorder. *Psychiatry and Clinical Neurosciences, 52*(S1). https://doi.org/10.1046/j.1440-1819.1998.0520s5083.x

12. De Bellis, M. D., & Thomas, L. A. (2003). Biologic findings of post-traumatic stress disorder and child maltreatment. *Current Psychiatry Reports, 5*(2), 108–117. https://doi.org/10.1007/s11920-003-0027-z

13. Wheeler, K. (2007). Psychotherapeutic strategies for healing trauma. *Perspectives in Psychiatric Care, 43*(3), 132–141. https://doi.org/10.1111/j.1744-6163.2007.00122.x

COMPASSION FOR COLLEAGUES

1. Great Circle. (2017, October). *A national and across-state profile on adverse childhood experiences among U.S. children and possibilities to heal and thrive.* https://www.greatcircle.org/images/pdfs/aces-brief-101717.pdf

2. Adams, R. E., Boscarino, J. A., & Figley, C. R. (2006). Compassion fatigue and psychological distress among social workers: A validation study. *American Journal of Orthopsychiatry, 76*(1), 103–108. https://doi.org/10.1037/0002-9432.76.1.103

3. The American Institute of Stress. (2017, January 4). *Compassion fatigue.* https://www.stress.org/military/for-practitionersleaders/compassion-fatigue

4. Roberts, D. (2018, June 20). *Why humans need connection.* Thrive Global. https://thriveglobal.com/stories/why-humans-need-connection/

CHAPTER 3: OVERCOMING

1. Seligman, M. E., Maier, S. F., & Geer, J. H. (1968). Alleviation of learned helplessness in the dog. *Journal of Abnormal Psychology, 73* (3, Pt. 1), 256–262. https://doi.org/10.1037/h0025831

2. Alloy, L. B., Peterson, C., Abramson, L. Y., & Seligman, M. E. (1984). Attributional style and the generality of learned helplessness. *Journal of Personality and Social Psychology, 46*(3), 681–687. https://doi.org/10.1037/0022-3514.46.3.681

3. Alloy, L. B., Peterson, C., Abramson, L. Y., & Seligman, M. E. (1984). Attributional style and the generality of learned helplessness. *Journal of Personality and Social Psychology, 46*(3), 681–687. https://doi.org/10.1037/0022-3514.46.3.681

4. Browne, C., & Winkelman, C. (2007). The effect of childhood trauma on later psychological adjustment. *Journal of Interpersonal Violence, 22*(6), 684–697. https://doi.org/10.1177/0886260507300207

5. Snyder, C. R. (2002). Hope theory: Rainbows in the mind. *Psychological Inquiry, 13*(4), 249–275. https://doi.org/10.1207/S15327965PLI1304_01

6. Gallagher, M. W., Marques, S. C., & Lopez, S. J. (2016). Hope and the academic trajectory of college students. *Journal of Happiness Studies, 18*(2), 341–352. https://doi.org/10.1007/s10902-016-9727-z

7. Hellman, C. M., & Gwinn, C. (2016). Camp HOPE as an intervention for children exposed to domestic violence: A program evaluation of hope, and strength of character. *Child and Adolescent Social Work Journal, 34*(3), 269–276. https://doi.org/10.1007/s10560-016-0460-6

8. Dixson, D. D., Keltner, D., Worrell, F. C., & Mello, Z. (2017). The magic of hope: Hope mediates the relationship between socioeconomic status and academic achievement. *The Journal of Educational Research, 111*(4), 507–515. https://doi.org/10.1080/00220671.2017.1302915

9. McGowan, S., & Felten, P. (2021). On the necessity of hope in academic development. *International Journal for Academic Development, 26*(4), 473–476. https://doi.org/10.1080/1360144x.2021.1903902

10. Wang, S., Xu, X., Zhou, M., Chen, T., Yang, X., Chen, G., & Gong, Q. (2017). Hope and the brain: Trait hope mediates the protective role of medial orbitofrontal cortex spontaneous activity against anxiety. *NeuroImage, 157*, 439–447. https://doi.org/10.1016/j.neuroimage.2017.05.056

11. Snyder, C. R., Hoza, B., Pelham, W. E., Rapoff, M., Ware, L., Danovsky, M., Highberger, L., Ribinstein, H., & Stahl, K. J. (1997). The development and validation of the Children's Hope Scale. *Journal of Pediatric Psychology, 22*(3), 399–421. https://doi.org/10.1093/jpepsy/22.3.399

12. Parker, P. D., Ciarrochi, J., Heaven, P., Marshall, S., Sahdra, B., & Kiuru, N. (2014). Hope, friends, and subjective well-being: Asocial network approach to peer group contextual effects. *Child Development, 86*(2), 642–650. https://doi.org/10.1111/cdev.12308

13. Krings, F., Bangerter, A., Gomez, V., & Grob, A. (2008). Cohort differences in personal goals and life satisfaction in young adulthood: Evidence for historical shifts in developmental tasks. *Journal of Adult Development, 15*(2), 93–105. https://doi.org/10.1007/s10804-008-9039-6

14. Cheavens, J. S., Heiy, J. E., Feldman, D. B., Benitez, C., & Rand, K. L. (2018). Hope, goals, and pathways: Further validating the hope scale with observer ratings. *The Journal of Positive Psychology, 14*(4), 452–462. https://doi.org/10.1080/17439760.2018.1484937

15. Lin, S., Fabris, M. A., & Longobardi, C. (2021, May 12). Closeness in student-teacher relationships and students' psychological well-being: The mediating role of hope. *Journal of Emotional and Behavioral Disorders*. https://doi.org/10.1177/10634266211013756

16. Ikeda, K., Kakinuma, K., Jiang, J., & Tanaka, A. (2021). Achievement goals affect memory encoding. *Contemporary Educational Psychology, 65*, 101945. https://doi.org/10.1016/j.cedpsych.2021.101945

17. Woolley, K., & Fishbach, A. (2018). It's about time: Earlier rewards increase intrinsic motivation. *Journal of Personality and Social Psychology, 114*(6), 877–890. https://doi.org/10.1037/pspa0000116

COMPASSION FOR COLLEAGUES

1. Gallup. (2018). *State of the American workplace: Employee engagement insights for U.S. business leaders.* www.gallup.com/file/services/176708/State_of_the_American_Workplace

2. Gallup. (2018). *State of the American workplace: Employee engagement insights for U.S. business leaders.* www.gallup.com/file/services/176708/State_of_the_American_Workplace

3. Li, Y. N., Law, K. S., & Yan, M. (2019). Other-caring or other-critical? A contagious effect of leaders' emotional triads on subordinates' performance. *Asia Pacific Journal of Management, 36*(4), 995–1021. https://doi.org/10.1007/s10490-018-9617-5

4. Li, Y. N., Law, K. S., & Yan, M. (2019). Other-caring or other-critical? A contagious effect of leaders' emotional triads on subordinates' performance. *Asia Pacific Journal of Management, 36*(4), 995–1021. https://doi.org/10.1007/s10490-018-9617-5

5. Ozyilmaz, A. (2019). Hope and human capital enhance job engagement to improve workplace outcomes. *Journal of Occupational and Organizational Psychology, 93*(1), 187–214. https://doi.org/10.1111/joop.12289

CHAPTER 4: PLANNING

1. Eun, B. (2017). The zone of proximal development as an overarching concept: A framework for synthesizing Vygotsky's theories. *Educational Philosophy and Theory, 51*(1), 18–30. https://doi.org/10.1080/00131857.2017.1421941

2. Duckworth, A. L., Peterson, C., Matthews, M. D., & Kelly, D. R. (2007). Grit: Perseverance and passion for long-term goals. *Journal of Personality and Social Psychology, 92*(6), 1087–1101. https://doi.org/10.1037/0022-3514.92.6.1087

3. Rand, K. L., & Cheavens, J. S. (2009). Hope theory. *The Oxford Handbook of Positive Psychology*, 322–334. https://doi.org/10.1093/oxfordhb/9780195187243.013.0030

4. Li, P. F., Wong, Y. J., McDermott, R. C., Cheng, H.-L., & Ruser, J. B. (2019). U.S. college students' lay

beliefs about hope: A mixed-methods study. *The Journal of Positive Psychology, 16*(2), 249–262. https://doi.org/10.1080/17439760.2019.1689420

5. Min, S., & Goff, P. T. (2016). The relations of a school's capacity for institutional diversity to student achievement in socio-economically, ethnically, and linguistically diverse schools. *International Journal of Inclusive Education, 20*(12), 1310–1325. https://doi.org/10.1080/13603116.2016.1168876

6. Karademas, E. C. (2006). Self-efficacy, social support, and well-being. *Personality and Individual Differences, 40*(6), 1281–1290. https://doi.org/10.1016/j.paid.2005.10.019

7. Allen, E. C., & Collisson, B. (2020). Do aspirational role models inspire or backfire? Perceived similarity mediates the effect of role models on minority students' college choices. *Journal of Marketing for Higher Education, 30*(2), 221–238. https://doi.org/10.1080/08841241.2020.1723780

8. Gopalan, V., Zulkifli, A. N., & Bakar, J. A. (2020). A review of motivation theories, models and instruments in learning environment. *Journal of Critical Reviews, 7*(6). https://doi.org/10.31838/jcr.07.06.100

9. Linley, P. A., & Joseph, S. (2004). Positive change following trauma and adversity: A review. *Journal of Traumatic Stress, 17*(1), 11–21. https://doi.org/10.1023/b:jots.0000014671.27856.7e

10. Moeller, A. J., Theiler, J. M., & Wu, C. (2012). Goal setting and student achievement: A longitudinal study. *The Modern Language Journal (Boulder, Colo.), 96*(2), 153–169. https://doi.org/10.1111/j.1540-4781.2011.01231.x

COMPASSION FOR COLLEAGUES

1. Zavelevsky, E., & Lishchinsky, O. S. (2020). An ecological perspective of teacher retention: An emergent model. *Teaching and Teacher Education, 88*, 102965. https://doi.org/10.1016/j.tate.2019.102965

2. Chrysikou, E. G., Motyka, K., Nigro, C., Yang, S.-I., & Thompson-Schill, S. L. (2016). Functional fixedness in creative thinking tasks depends on stimulus modality. *Psychology of Aesthetics,*

Creativity, and the Arts, 10(4), 425–435. https://doi.org/10.1037/aca0000050

3. Witvliet, C. V., Richie, F. J., Root Luna, L. M., & Van Tongeren, D. R. (2018). Gratitude predicts hope and happiness: A two-study assessment of traits and states. *The Journal of Positive Psychology, 14*(3), 271–282. https://doi.org/10.1080/17439760.2018.1424924

4. Croke, L. (2019). Cultivating gratitude can lead to mental, physical, and work-related benefits. *AORN Journal, 110*(5). https://doi.org/10.1002/aorn.12871

5. Croke, L. (2019). Cultivating gratitude can lead to mental, physical, and work-related benefits. *AORN Journal, 110*(5). https://doi.org/10.1002/aorn.12871

CHAPTER 5: ENERGIZING

1. Dixson, D. D. (2019). Hope into action: How clusters of hope relate to success-oriented behavior in school. *Psychology in the Schools, 56*(9), 1493–1511. https://doi.org/10.1002/pits.22299

2. Tangney, J. P., Baumeister, R. F., & Boone, A. L. (2004). High self-control predicts good adjustment, less pathology, better grades, and interpersonal success. *Journal of Personality, 72*(2), 271–324. https://doi.org/10.1111/j.0022-3506.2004.00263.x

3. Hattie, J. (2015). The applicability of visible learning to higher education. *Scholarship of Teaching and Learning in Psychology, 1*(1), 79–91. https://doi.org/10.1037/stl0000021

4. Yarcheski, A., & Mahon, N. E. (2014). Meta-analyses of predictors of hope in adolescents. *Western Journal of Nursing Research, 38*(3), 345–368. https://doi.org/10.1177/0193945914559545

5. Ent, M. R., Baumeister, R. F., & Tice, D. M. (2015). Trait self-control and the avoidance of temptation. *Personality and Individual Differences, 74,* 12–15. https://doi.org/10.1016/j.paid.2014.09.031

6. Woolley, K., & Fishbach, A. (2016). For the fun of it: Harnessing immediate rewards to increase persistence in long-term goals. *Journal of Consumer Research, 42*(6), 952–966. https://doi.org/10.1093/jcr/ucv098

7. Deci, E. L., Koestner, R., & Ryan, R. M. (1999). A meta-analytic review of experiments examining the effects of extrinsic rewards on intrinsic motivation. *Psychological Bulletin, 125*(6), 627–668. https://doi.org/10.1037/0033-2909.125.6.627

8. Soutschek, A., Ugazio, G., Crockett, M. J., Ruff, C. C., Kalenscher, T., & Tobler, P. N. (2017). Binding oneself to the mast: Stimulating frontopolar cortex enhances precommitment. *Social Cognitive and Affective Neuroscience, 12*(4), 635–642. https://doi.org/10.1093/scan/nsw176

9. van Dillen, L. F., Papies, E. K., & Hofmann, W. (2013). Turning a blind eye to temptation: How cognitive load can facilitate self-regulation. *Journal of Personality and Social Psychology, 104*(3), 427–443. https://doi.org/10.1037/a0031262

10. Shapiro, S. L., Oman, D., Thoresen, C. E., Plante, T. G., & Flinders, T. (2008). Cultivating mindfulness: Effects on well-being. *Journal of Clinical Psychology, 64*(7), 840–862. https://doi.org/10.1002/jclp.20491

11. van Dillen, L. F., & Papies, E. K. (2014). From distraction to mindfulness: Psychological and neural mechanisms of attention strategies in self-regulation. In G. H. E. Gendolla, M. Tops, & S. L. Koole (Eds.), *Handbook of biobehavioral approaches to self-regulation* (pp. 141–154). https://doi.org/10.1007/978-1-4939-1236-0_10

12. Webb, T. L., & Sheeran, P. (2007). How do implementation intentions promote goal attainment? A test of component processes. *Journal of Experimental Social Psychology, 43*(2), 295–302. https://doi.org/10.1016/j.jesp.2006.02.001

13. Lally, P., Van Jaarsveld, C. H., Potts, H. W., & Wardle, J. (2009). How are habits formed: Modeling habit formation in the real world. *European Journal of Social Psychology, 40*(6), 998–1009. https://doi.org/10.1002/ejsp.674

14. Veilleux, J. C., Skinner, K. D., Baker, D. E., & Chamberlain, K. D. (2021). Perceived willpower self-efficacy fluctuates dynamically with affect and distress intolerance. *Journal of Research in Personality, 90,* 104058. https://doi.org/10.1016/j.jrp.2020.104058

15. Schnall, S., Zadra, J. R., & Proffitt, D. R. (2010). Direct evidence for the economy of action: Glucose and

the perception of geographical slant. *Perception, 39*(4), 464–482. https://doi.org/10.1068/p6445

16. Riener, C. R., Stefanucci, J. K., Proffitt, D. R., & Clore, G. (2010). An effect of mood on the perception of geographical slant. *Cognition and Emotion, 25*(1), 174–182. https://doi.org/10.1080/02699931003738026

17. Schnall, S., Harber, K. D., Stefanucci, J. K., & Proffitt, D. R. (2008). Social support and the perception of geographical slant. *Journal of Experimental Social Psychology, 44*(5), 1246–1255. https://doi.org/10.1016/j.jesp.2008.04.011

18. Bhalla, M., & Proffitt, D. R. (1999). Visual-motor recalibration in geographical slant perception. *Journal of Experimental Psychology: Human Perception and Performance, 25*(4), 1076–1096. https://doi.org/10.1037/0096-1523.25.4.1076

19. Gong, S., & Li, Q. (2016). Rebuilding self-control after ego depletion: The role of positive emotions. *Advances in Intelligent Systems and Computing*, 1401–1411. https://doi.org/10.1007/978-981-10-1837-4_113

20. Tice, D. M., Baumeister, R. F., Shmueli, D., & Muraven, M. (2007). Restoring the self: Positive affect helps improve self-regulation following ego depletion. *Journal of Experimental Social Psychology, 43*(3), 379–384. https://doi.org/10.1016/j.jesp.2006.05.007

21. Carlson, K. A. (2011). The impact of humor on memory: Is the humor effect about humor? *Humor—International Journal of Humor Research, 24*(1). https://doi.org/10.1515/humr.2011.002

22. Banas, J. A., Dunbar, N., Rodriguez, D., & Liu, S.-J. (2011). A review of humor in educational settings: Four decades of research. *Communication Education, 60*(1), 115–144. https://doi.org/10.1080/03634523.2010.496867

COMPASSION FOR COLLEAGUES

1. Müller, K., Alliata, R., & Benninghoff, F. (2009). Attracting and retaining teachers. *Educational Management Administration & Leadership, 37*(5), 574–599. https://doi.org/10.1177/1741143209339651

CHAPTER 6: THE SCHOOL OF HOPE

1. American Academy of Pediatrics. (2021, October). *Declaration of a national emergency in child and adolescent mental health*. Centers for Disease Control and Prevention. https://www.aap.org/en/advocacy/child-and-adolescent-healthy-mental-development/aap-aacap-cha-declaration-of-a-national-emergency-in-child-and-adolescent-mental-health/

2. Fowler, J. H., & Christakis, N. A. (2008). Dynamic spread of happiness in a large social network: Longitudinal analysis over 20 years in the Framingham Heart Study. *BMJ, 337*(2). https://doi.org/10.1136/bmj.a2338

INDEX

A SAGE Publishing Company

Helping educators make the greatest impact

CORWIN HAS ONE MISSION: to enhance education through intentional professional learning.

We build long-term relationships with our authors, educators, clients, and associations who partner with us to develop and continuously improve the best evidence-based practices that establish and support lifelong learning.

Keep learning...

Also from Cathleen Beachboard

HOPE TEACHER CERTIFICATION

Become a Hope Certified Teacher

In partnership with Thrively, Cathleen Beachboard has designed a research-driven, evidence-based certification program for teachers who want to instill hope in every learner they serve. This certification is specifically designed with educators in mind thanks to Cathleen's personal experience as a teacher herself.

FREE HOPE PLAYLIST

Instill Hope in Your Classroom

Explore Cathleen's easy-to-use Hope Playlist on Thrively. This playlist is designed to help students develop goal-directed thinking that uses both pathways (the capacity to find routes to their desired goals) and agency (the necessary motivation to use those routes).

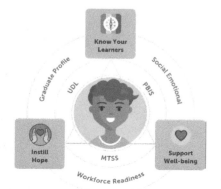

MORE ABOUT THRIVELY

Thrively believes every child has a genius and deserves to thrive. They are on a mission to ensure every learner is known, develops a positive learning identity, has their well-being supported, and is instilled with hope, no matter their background or circumstances.

Visit **thrively.com/classroom** to learn more about how Thrively can help you unleash the genius in every child.